The UNOFFICIAL Book of Political Lists

Also by Iain Dale and published by Robson Books

As I Said to Denis . . .
The Margaret Thatcher Book of Quotations

The Blair Necessities
The Tony Blair Book of Quotations

The UNOFFICIAL Book of Political Lists

Iain Dale

Robson Books

First published in Great Britain in 1997 by Robson Books Ltd, Bolsover House, 5-6 Clipstone Street, London W1P 8LE

British Library Cataloguing in Publication Data
A catalogue record for this title is available from the British Library

ISBN 1 86105 110 7

Set in Palatino by Derek Doyle & Associates, Mold, Flintshire.
Printed in Great Britain by Creative Print & Design Ltd., Ebbw Vale, S. Wales.

For
Sheena & Tracey

Contents

Part 1 Parliament and Government

Part 2 Elections and Voting

Part 3 Parties and Policies

A Ten-point Transport Policy for the Next Government (Unofficial)
Ten Things Which Should Be Against the Law But Aren't (Unofficial)
Top Ten Rejected Names for the Liberal Democrats (Unofficial)

Part 4 World Politics

Eight Austrian Chancellors Since 1945
Eleven Belgian Prime Ministers Since 1961
Nine Danish Prime Ministers Since 1960
Seven French Presidents Since 1947
Sixteen French Prime Ministers Since 1958
Six German Chancellors Since 1949
Fifteen Irish Prime Ministers Since 1932
Twenty-Six Italian Prime Ministers Since 1959
Ten Dutch Prime Ministers Since 1959
Eight Russian and Soviet Heads of Government Since 1922
Seven Spanish Prime Ministers Since 1939
Nine Swedish Prime Ministers Since 1946
Nine Longest-serving World Leaders
First Ten Female Presidents and Prime Ministers
Twenty-Six Women Politicians Who Have Become Party Leader, Prime
   Minister or President
Names of Parliaments Abroad
Top Ten US Presidents
Bottom Ten US Presidents
Eight American Presidents to Die in Office
US Presidents with Most Electoral College Votes
US Presidents with Highest Popular Votes
Oldest US Presidents (at Inauguration)
Youngest US Presidents (at Inauguration)
Eleven Canadian Prime Ministers Since 1935
Four Chinese Prime Ministers since 1949
Ten Indian Prime Ministers Since 1949
Thirteen New Zealand Prime Ministers Since 1940
Twelve Israeli Prime Ministers Since 1948
Fifteen Japanese Prime Ministers Since 1960
Eleven Australian Prime Ministers Since 1945

Part 5 General Politics

Part 6 Quotations

Part 7 Sex, Money and Scandal

Part 8 More Unofficial Lists (The Funny Part!)

Acknowledgements

Most people think of political reference books as either dead boring or prohibitively expensive. Hopefully this is neither – but then again it is rather more than a reference book. Where in *Dod's Parliamentary Companion* could the reader find the Top Ten Political Chat-Up Lines alongside a List of Prime Ministers Since 1721? So this book is all about information and fun – two words not always associated with political life.

It is easy to be sceptical of politicians and to believe that they're all the same and are only in politics for what they can get out of it. The truth is somewhat more simple. Our politicians reflect the society in which we live. Proportionately there are no more crooked politicians than there are crooked bank managers (perhaps a poor comparison, but there you go!) Politicians are no more likely to sleep around than journalists, although one could be forgiven for thinking otherwise. Generally speaking, politicians of all parties are honourable people who genuinely wish to improve the life of the people, while continuously disagreeing with each other about how to go about it. But that's democracy. And that's what this book is all about. Where else but in a true democracy could you read in a book the Top Ten Politicians Gay Men Find Attractive?

I would like to thank the publishers of this book, Robson Books, and in particular Jeremy Robson, Kate Mills and Charlotte Bush. A full bibliography of source materials is listed at the end of the book and I am grateful to all those who have kindly given permission for their words to be used.

The most difficult part of writing and compiling this book has been to put the more than 300 lists into a logical and easily accessible order. I have decided to divide it into eight sections, finishing with the humorous bit! However, in order for the reader not to become submerged by fact and information there is also a scattering of 'unofficial' lists throughout the book – easily recognisable by the stamp which appears on the page.

In many ways this book could well be over a thousand pages in length. We have cut it down to a manageable size, but that has entailed leaving out many highly entertaining and informative lists. Should Robson Books in their wisdom decide to ask me to compile a second volume in the future they will no doubt be included there. Should you, the reader, be inspired, please do feel free to send me ideas for future political lists (fact or fiction). Any lists I receive which are complete and then published will receive full acknowledgement. Please send them to me at Robson Books, 5–6 Clipstone Street, London, W1.

I hope reading this book gives you as much enjoyment as compiling it gave me.

Iain Dale

Part One

Parliament
and
Government

British Prime Ministers 1721 to the present

	1997–	Tony Blair
	1990–7	John Major
	1979–0	Margaret Thatcher
	1976–9	James Callaghan
	1974–6	Harold Wilson
	1970–4	Edward Heath
	1964–70	Harold Wilson
34	1963–4	Alec Douglas-Home
33	1957–63	Harold Macmillan
32	1955–7	Anthony Eden
	1951–5	Winston Churchill
	1945–51	Clement Attlee
	1940–5	Winston Churchill
	1937–40	Neville Chamberlain
	1935–7	Stanley Baldwin
	1929–35	Ramsay MacDonald
	1924–9	Stanley Baldwin
	1924	Ramsay MacDonald
	1923–4	Stanley Baldwin
	1922–3	Andrew Bonar Law
	1916–22	David Lloyd George
	1908–16	Herbert Asquith
	1905–8	Henry Campbell-Bannerman
	1902–5	Arthur Balfour
21	1895–1902	Marquess of Salisbury
	1894–5	Earl of Rosebery
	1892–4	William Ewart Gladstone
	1886–92	Marquess of Salisbury
	1886	William Ewart Gladstone
20	1885–6	Marquess of Salisbury
	1880–5	William Ewart Gladstone
	1874–80	Benjamin Disraeli
19	1868–74	William Ewart Gladstone
	1868	Benjamin Disraeli

	1866–8	Earl of Derby
	1865–6	Earl Russell
	1859–65	Viscount Palmerston
	1858–9	Earl of Derby
	1855–8	Viscount Palmerston
	1852–5	Earl of Aberdeen
15	1852	Earl of Derby
	1846–52	Lord John Russell
	1841–6	Robert Peel
	1835–41	Viscount Melbourne
13	1834–5	Robert Peel
	1834	Viscount Melbourne
12	1832–4	Earl Grey
11	1832	Duke of Wellington
	1830–2	Earl Grey
	1828–30	Duke of Wellington
	1827–8	Viscount Goderich
9	1827	George Canning
	1812–27	Lord Liverpool
	1809–12	Spencer Perceval
	1807–9	Duke of Portland
6	1806–7	Lord Grenville
	1804–6	William Pitt the Younger
	1801–4	Henry Addington
	1783–1801	William Pitt the Younger
	1783	Duke of Portland
	1782–3	Earl of Shelburne
	1782	Marquis of Rockingham
	1770–82	Lord North
	1766–70	Duke of Grafton
	1765–6	Marquis of Rockingham
	1763–5	George Grenville
	1762–3	Earl of Bute
	1757–62	Duke of Newcastle
	1757	Earl Waldegrave
	1756–7	Duke of Devonshire
	1754–6	Duke of Newcastle
	1746–54	Henry Pelham
	1746	Earl of Bath
	1743–6	Henry Pelham

4

| 1742–3 | Earl of Wilmington |
| 1721–42 | Robert Walpole |

Sixteen Prime Ministers Born in London

Duke of Newcastle	Lord Melbourne
George Grenville	Lord John Russell
Earl of Chatham	Lord Palmerston
Lord North	Benjamin Disraeli
Henry Addington	Lord Rosebery
Spencer Perceval	Clement Attlee
Earl of Liverpool	Harold Macmillan
George Canning	Alec Douglas Home

Five Prime Ministers Born in Scotland

Earl of Bute	Henry Campbell-Bannerman
Earl of Aberdeen	Ramsay MacDonald
Arthur Balfour	

Four Prime Ministers with No Siblings

Earl of Liverpool	Ramsay MacDonald
Stanley Baldwin	Tony Blair

Ten Prime Ministers Who Married Twice

Robert Walpole	Lord John Russell
Duke of Grafton	Earl of Aberdeen
Earl of Shelburne	Henry Asquith
Henry Addington	David Lloyd George
Earl of Liverpool	Anthony Eden

Eleven Prime Ministers Who Had No Children

Earl of Wilmington
Duke of Newcastle
Marquess of Rockingham
William Pitt
Lord Grenville
Earl of Liverpool

Lord Palmerston
Benjamin Disraeli
Arthur Balfour
Henry Campbell-Bannerman
Edward Heath

Twenty Longest-serving Prime Ministers Since 1721

1.	Robert Walpole	20 yrs 10 months
2.	William Pitt the Younger	18 yrs 11 months
3.	Lord Liverpool	14 yrs 8 months
4.	Marquess of Salisbury	13 yrs 9 months
5.	William Ewart Gladstone	12 yrs 5 months
6.	Lord North	12 yrs 1 month
7.	Margaret Thatcher	11 yrs 6 months
8.	Henry Pelham	10 yrs 7 months
9.	Viscount Palmerston	9 yrs 4 months
10.	Herbert Asquith	8 yrs 8 months
11.	Winston Churchill	8 yrs 7 months
12.	Harold Wilson	7 yrs 9 months
13.	Duke of Newcastle	7 yrs 7 months
14.	Stanley Baldwin	7 yrs 2 months
15.	Benjamin Disraeli	6 yrs 11 months
16.	Ramsay MacDonald	6 yrs 9 months
17.	Harold Macmillan	6 yrs 9 months
18.	Lord Melbourne	6 yrs 8 months
19.	John Major	6 yrs 5 months
20.	Lord John Russell	6 yrs 3 months

Length of Service of Twentieth-century Prime Ministers

Marquess of Salisbury	13 yrs 9 months
Margaret Thatcher	11 yrs 6 months
Herbert Asquith	8 yrs 8 months
Winston Churchill	8 yrs 8 months
Harold Wilson	7 yrs 9 months
Stanley Baldwin	7 yrs 2 months
Ramsay MacDonald	6 yrs 9 months
Harold Macmillan	6 yrs 9 months
John Major	6 yrs 5 months
Clement Attlee	6 yrs 3 months
David Lloyd George	5 yrs 10 months
Edward Heath	3 yrs 8 months
Arthur Balfour	3 yrs 5 months
James Callaghan	3 yrs 1 month
Neville Chamberlain	2 yrs 11 months
Henry Campbell-Bannerman	2 yrs 4 months
Anthony Eden	1 yr 9 months
Alec Douglas-Home	1 yr
Andrew Bonar Law	7 months

Ten Shortest-serving Prime Ministers

1.	George Canning	119 days
2.	Viscount Goderich	130 days
3.	Andrew Bonar Law	209 days
4.	Duke of Devonshire	225 days
5.	Earl of Shelburne	266 days
6.	Earl of Bute	317 days
7.	Alec Douglas-Home	363 days
8.	Lord Grenville	1 yr 42 days
9.	Duke of Grafton	1 yr 106 days
10.	Lord Rosebery	1 yr 109 days

Twenty-Three Politicians Who Became Prime Minister More Than Once

4	William Ewart Gladstone	2	William Pitt
4	Marquess of Salisbury	2	Duke of Wellington
4	Herbert Asquith	2	Lord Melbourne
4	Ramsay MacDonald	2	Robert Peel
4	Stanley Baldwin	2	Lord John Russell
4	Harold Wilson	2	Duke of Palmerston
3	Earl of Derby	2	Benjamin Disraeli
3	Winston Churchill	2	Lloyd George
3	Margaret Thatcher	2	Clement Attlee
2	Duke of Newcastle	2	Harold Macmillan
2	Earl of Rockingham	2	John Major
2	Duke of Portland		

Eight Deputy Prime Ministers

The post of Deputy Prime Minister does not officially exist. It is entirely at the discretion of the Prime Minister whether a deputy is appointed. Winston Churchill led the way by appointing his coalition partner as his deputy during the war.

Clement Attlee	1942–5
Herbert Morrison	1945–51
Anthony Eden	1951–5
R A Butler	1962–3
William Whitelaw	1979–88
Geoffrey Howe	1989–90
Michael Heseltine	1995–7
John Prescott	1997–

Eleven Prime Ministers Who Did Not Attend University

Duke of Devonshire
Earl of Rockingham
Duke of Wellington
Benjamin Disraeli
David Lloyd George
Andrew Bonar Law

Ramsay MacDonald
Neville Chamberlain
Winston Churchill
James Callaghan
John Major

Twenty-Five Prime Ministers Who Attended Oxford University

George Grenville
Earl of Shelburne
Earl of Wilmington
Henry Pelham
Duke of Portland
Lord Grenville
Earl of Chatham
Lord North
Lord Addington
Earl of Liverpool
George Canning
Robert Peel
Earl of Derby

William Gladstone
Lord Salisbury
Lord Rosebery
Henry Asquith
Clement Attlee
Anthony Eden
Harold Macmillan
Alec Douglas-Home
Harold Wilson
Edward Heath
Margaret Thatcher
Tony Blair

Thirteen Prime Ministers Who Attended Cambridge University

Robert Walpole
Duke of Newcastle
William Pitt
Duke of Grafton
Spencer Perceval
Viscount Goderich
Earl Grey

Lord Melbourne
Earl of Aberdeen
Lord Palmerston
Arthur Balfour
Henry Campbell-Bannerman
Stanley Baldwin

Seven Prime Ministers Who Died in Office

Earl of Wilmington   Spencer Perceval
Henry Pelham   George Canning
Earl of Rockingham   Lord Palmerston
William Pitt

Eight Prime Ministers Never Awarded a Peerage

George Grenville   Andrew Bonar Law
Robert Peel   Ramsay MacDonald
William Gladstone   Neville Chamberlain
Henry Campbell-Bannerman   Winston Churchill

NB Edward Heath and John Major still sit in the House of Commons

Four Prime Ministers Who Fought Duels

Earl of Shelburne   George Canning
William Pitt   Duke of Wellington

Ten Prime Ministers Injured in Accidents

Lord North	Broke his arm in 1776 after falling from his horse
Earl of Chatham	Fell off his horse in 1777 following a stroke
Duke of Portland	Suffered a dislocated collar bone and a fractured rib in a riding accident in 1782
George Canning	Injured leg in riding accident in 1804
Earl of Bute	Fell down a cliff while collecting plants
Earl Grey	Injured from a falling picture frame
William Gladstone	Lost the top of his left forefinger in a shooting incident
Ramsay MacDonald	Knocked down by a bicycle

| Harold Macmillan | Knocked down by a taxi |
| John Major | Injured his knee in a car accident in Nigeria |

Ten Prime Ministers on the Fast Track

The average span of time between a Prime Minister first entering Parliament and being appointed Prime Minister is about twenty-five years. There follows a list of those who achieved the highest office in the land the quickest. . .

1.	William Pitt	2 yrs	6.	Tony Blair	13
2.	Lord Addington	6	7.	Earl of Rockingham	14
3.	John Major	11	8.	Stanley Baldwin	15
4.	Duke of Grafton	11	9.	Duke of Devonshire	15
5.	Spencer Perceval	13	10.	Lord North	15

Ten Prime Ministers on the Slow Track

This list shows the Tortoise PMs – those who took years and years to reach the highest Office in the land. . .

1.	Lord Palmerston	47 yrs
2.	Earl of Aberdeen	46
3.	Earl Grey	44
4.	Earl of Wilmington	43
5.	Duke of Newcastle	39
6.	Winston Churchill	39
7.	Henry Campbell-Bannerman	37
8.	William Gladstone	35
9.	George Canning	33
10.	Lord John Russell	32

Eleven Prime Ministers Who Served Longest in the House of Commons

1.	Winston Churchill	63 yrs		7.	Edward Heath	47*
2.	William Gladstone	62		8.	Alec Douglas-Home	42
3.	Lord Palmerston	58		9.	James Callaghan	41
4.	Lloyd George	54		10.	Robert Peel	41
5.	Arthur Balfour	48		11.	Robert Walpole	41
6.	Lord John Russell	47				

* Edward Heath is still serving as a Member of the House of Commons.

Ten Youngest Prime Ministers

1.	24 yrs	William Pitt the Younger
2.	33	Duke of Grafton
3.	35	Earl of Rockingham
4.	36	Duke of Devonshire
5.	37	Lord North
6.	42	Earl of Liverpool
7.	43	Lord Addington
8.	43	Tony Blair
9.	44	Robert Walpole
10.	44	Viscount Goderich

Nine Oldest Prime Ministers Upon Leaving Office

80	William Gladstone	
80	Lord Palmerston	72 Lord Salisbury
80	Winston Churchill	71 Duke of Portland
75	Benjamin Disraeli	71 Henry Campbell-Bannerman
73	Earl Russell	71 Neville Chamberlain

Ten Oldest Politicians to Have Been Appointed Prime Minister

82 William Gladstone
76 Winston Churchill
75 ~~Duke of~~ Palmerston
73 Lord John Russell
69 Duke of Portland
69 Henry Campbell-Bannerman
69 Benjamin Disraeli
69 Earl of Wilmington
68 Earl of Aberdeen
68 Neville Chamberlain

Zodiac Signs of British Prime Ministers

Aries	6	North, Portland, Canning, Derby, Callaghan, Major
Libra	6	Pelham, George Grenville, Grafton, Palmerston, MacDonald, Thatcher
Gemini	5	Bute, Pitt, Addington, Liverpool, Eden
Pisces	5	Rockingham, Grey, Melbourne, Chamberlain, Wilson
Aquarius	4	Peel, Aberdeen, Salisbury, Macmillan
Scorpio	4	Chatham, Lord Grenville, Perceval, Goderich
Taurus	4	Shelburne, Wellington, Rosebery, Blair
Virgo	4	Walpole, Campbell-Bannerman, Asquith, Bonar Law
Cancer	3	Newcastle, Douglas-Home, Heath
Capricorn	3	Gladstone, Lloyd George, Attlee
Leo	3	Russell, Balfour, Baldwin
Sagittarius	2	Disraeli, Churchill

(The list excludes Wilmington and Devonshire whose exact birth dates are not known)

Ten Longest Living Prime Ministers

1.	Harold Macmillan	92		6.	Lord John Russell	85
2.	Winston Churchill	90		7.	Clement Attlee	84
3.	William Gladstone	88		8.	Duke of Wellington	83
4.	Alec Douglas-Home	87		9.	David Lloyd George	82
5.	Henry Addington	86		10.	Lord Rosebery	82

Prime Ministers' Last Words

Harold Macmillan: 'I think I will go to sleep now.'

Neville Chamberlain: 'Approaching dissolution brings relief.'

Stanley Baldwin: 'I am ready.'

David Lloyd George: 'The sign of the cross, the sign of the cross.'

Henry Campbell-Bannerman: 'This is not the end of me.'

William Gladstone: 'Amen.'

Benjamin Disraeli: 'I had rather live but I am not afraid to die.'

Lord Palmerston: 'That's Article 98, now go on to the next' (thinking he was signing a treaty).

Earl of Derby: 'Bored to utter extinction.'

Duke of Wellington: 'Yes, if you please' (when offered a cup of tea).

Spencer Perceval: 'Oh, I am murdered.'

William Pitt: 'Oh my country, how I leave my country.'

Earl of Chatham: 'Leave your Father, and go to the defence of your country' (to his son, William Pitt).

Stages of a Bill's Progress to Becoming an Act of Parliament

First Reading (House of Commons)

Second Reading

Standing Committee

Report Stage

Third Reading

First Reading (House of Lords)

Second Reading

Committee Stage
Report Stage
Third Reading
Consideration of Lords Amendments (House of Commons)
Royal Assent

Twentieth Century Speakers of the House of Commons

1992	Betty Boothroyd	1951–9	W Morrison
1983–92	Bernard Weatherill	1943–51	D Clifton Brown
1976–83	George Thomas	1928–43	E Fitzroy
1971–6	Selwyn Lloyd	1921–8	J Whitley
1965–71	Horace King	1905–21	J Lowther – *OE*
1959–65	H Hylton-Foster	1895–1905	W Gully

Fathers of the House Since 1944

The Father of the House of Commons is the Member with the longest uninterrupted service. The current Father of the House, Edward Heath, was first elected in 1950.

1992–	Edward Heath	1964–5	R A Butler
1987–92	Bernard Braine	1959–64	Winston Churchill
1983–7	James Callaghan	1952–9	D Grenfell
1979–83	J Parker	1951–2	H O'Neill
1974–9	G Strauss	1944–51	Earl Winterton
1965–74	R Turton		

Votes of No Confidence Since 1976

Date	Government	Opposition	Subject
9 June 1976	309	290	Economy
23 March 1977	322	298	General
20 July 1977	312	282	Economy
14 December 1978	300	290	Economy
28 March 1979	310	311	General
28 February 1980	327	268	Economy
27 July 1981	331	262	Economy
28 October 1981	312	250	Economy
31 January 1985	395	222	Economy
22 November 1990	367	247	Resignation of Margaret Thatcher
27 March 1991	358	238	Community Charge
24 September 1992	322	296	Economy
23 July 1993	339	299	Europe

Emergency Recalls of the House of Commons Since 1945

September 1949	Devaluation
September 1950	Korean War
October 1951	Dissolution
September 1956	Suez Crisis
September 1959	Dissolution
October 1961	Berlin Wall Crisis
January 1968	Expenditure Cuts
August 1968	Czechoslovakia and Nigeria
May 1970	Dissolution
September 1971	Northern Ireland
January 1974	Fuel Crisis
June 1974	Northern Ireland
April 1982	Falklands Crisis
September 1990	Kuwait
September 1992	Exchange Rate Policy

Eight Cabinet Secretaries Since 1916

1997	Richard Wilson	1963	B Trend
1987	Robin Butler	1947	N Brook
1979	Robert Armstrong	1938	E Bridges
1973	John Hunt	1916	M Hankey

Eight Heads of the Number 10 Policy Unit

1997	David Miliband	1984	John Redwood
1993	Norman Blackwell	1982	Ferdinand Mount
1990	Sarah Hogg	1979	John Hoskyns
1985	Brian Griffiths	1974	Bernard Donoghue

British Members of the European Commission

1995	Leon Brittan and Neil Kinnock
1989	Leon Brittan and Bruce Millan
1985	Lord Cockfield and Stanley Clinton Davis
1981	Christopher Tugendhat and Ivor Richard
1977	Roy Jenkins and Christopher Tugendhat
1973	Christopher Soames and G Thomson

Eleven Ministers Responsible for European Affairs Since 1974

1997	Doug Henderson	1983	Malcolm Rifkind
1994	David Davis	1979	Douglas Hurd
1993	David Heathcoat-Amory	1977	Frank Judd
1990	Tristan Garel-Jones	1976	David Owen
1989	Francis Maude	1974	Roy Hattersley
1986	Lynda Chalker		

Fifteen Peers Who Have Renounced Their Titles

1963   Viscount Stansgate (Anthony Wedgwood Benn)
1963   Lord Altrincham (John Grigg)
1963   Earl of Home (Alec Douglas-Home)
1963   Viscount Hailsham (Quintin Hogg)
1964   Lord Southampton (E Fitzroy)
1964   Lord Monkswell (W Collier)
1964   Lord Beaverbrook (Max Aitken)
1964   Earl of Sandwich (V Montagu)
1966   Lord Fraser of Allander (Hugh Fraser)
1970   Earl of Durham (A Lambton)
1971   Lord Sanderson of Ayot (A Sanderson)
1972   Lord Reith (C Reith)
1973   Lord Silkin (A Silkin)
1975   Lord Archibald (G Archibald)
1977   Lord Merthyr (T Lewis)

Twelve Downing Street Press Secretaries Since 1964

1997	Alastair Campbell	1974	Joe Haines
1996	Jonathan Haslam	1973	W Haydon
1994	Christopher Meyer	1970	Donald Maitland
1990	Gus MacDonald	1969	Joe Haines
1979	Bernard Ingham	1964	Trevor Lloyd-Hughes
1976	Tom McCaffery	1957	Harold Evans

Ten Longest-serving MPs This Century

62	Winston Churchill	47	J Parker
54	David Lloyd George	47	J Gretton
49	G Lambert	47	H Chaplin
49	T P O'Connor	47	Edward Heath*
48	Arthur Balfour	46	Earl Winterton

* If Edward Heath lives until the millennium he will overtake G Lambert.

Fourteen Wives Who Have Inherited Their Husband's Seat This Century

1990   Irene Adams (Paisley North)
1986   Llin Golding (Newcastle under Lyne)
1982   Helen McElhone (Glasgow Queens Park)
1957   Lady Gammans (Hornsey)
1953   Lena Jeger (Holborn and St Pancras)
1943   Lady Apsley
1941   B Rathbone (Bodmin)
1937   Lady Davidson (Hemel Hempstead)
1937   A Hardie (Glasgow Springburn)
1930   Lady Noel-Buxton (North Norfolk)
1927   Countess of Iveagh (Southend)
1923   H Philipson (Berwick on Tweed)
1921   M Wintringham (Louth)
1919   Lady Astor (Plymouth Sutton)

Nine Oldest MPs This Century

96	S Young (1918)	86	J Collings (1918)
92	D Logan (1964)	86	S Chapman (1945)
89	Winston Churchill (1964)	85	S Davies (1972)
88	W Thorne (1945)	85	Emanuel Shinwell (1970)
87	R Cameron (1913)		

Eight Youngest MPs This Century

TDURNOUR

21	Viscount Turner (1904)	21	E Harmsworth (1919)
21	J Esmonde (1915)	21	H Lucas Tooth (1924)
21	P Whitty (1916)	21	P Clarke (1955)
21	J Sweeney (1918)	21	Bernadette Devlin (1969)

Ten Occasions When a Son or Daughter Has Succeeded a Parent

1987 Hilary Armstrong (Durham NW)
1970 Greville Janner (Leicester NW)
1959 Paul Channon (Southend West)
1953 P Ford (Down North)
1945 G Lambert (South Molton)
1914 Austen Chamberlain (Birmingham)
1913 P Meehan (Queens Co)
1913 R McCalmont (Antrim East)
1909 T Lundon (Limerick East)
1908 Stanley Baldwin (Bewdley)

Women in Parliament

	Conservative		Labour		LibDem		Other		Total	
	Cand	MPs	Cand	MPs	Cand	MPs	Cand	MPs	Cand	MPs
1918	1	0	4	0	4	0	8	1	17	1
1922	5	1	10	0	16	1	2	0	33	2
1923	7	3	14	3	12	2	1	0	34	8
1924	12	3	22	1	6	0	1	0	41	4
1929	10	3	30	9	25	1	4	1	69	14
1931	16	13	36	0	6	1	4	1	62	15
1935	19	6	35	1	11	1	2	1	67	9
1945	14	1	45	21	20	1	8	1	87	24
1950	28	6	42	14	45	1	11	0	126	21
1951	29	6	39	11	11	0	0	0	79	17
1955	32	10	43	14	12	0	2	0	89	24
1959	28	12	36	13	16	0	1	0	81	25
1964	24	11	33	18	25	0	8	0	90	29
1966	21	7	30	19	20	0	9	0	80	26
1970	26	15	29	10	23	0	21	1	99	26
1974 Feb	33	9	40	13	40	0	30	1	143	23
1974 Oct	30	7	50	18	49	0	32	2	161	27

	Conservative		Labour		LibDem		Other		Total	
	Cand	MPs	Cand	MPs	Cand	MPs	Cand	MPs	Cand	MPs
1979	31	8	52	11	51	0	76	0	210	19
1983	40	13	78	10	115	0	87	0	320	23
1987	46	17	92	21	106	2	85	1	329	41
1992	59	20	138	37	144	2	227	1	568	60
1997	67	12	159	101	122	3	34*	3	382*	119

* Figures for other candidates in the 1997 election have not yet been calculated to include all the minor party women candidates.

History of MPs' Pay

1912   MPs receive first ever salary of £400 p.a.

1913   £100 of MPs' salaries made tax exempt in lieu of expenses. This remained the case until 1954.

1924   MPs allowed free rail travel between London and their constituencies.

1931   Salaries are cut to £360 as an austerity measure.

1934   Salary restored to £380 and then to £400 in 1935.

1937   MPs are awarded a 50% pay rise taking their salaries to £600 p.a.

1946   Salaries are increased to £1,000. Free travel allowed also between MPs' homes and Westminster.

1953   A sessional allowance of £2 per sitting day (except Fridays) was introduced.

1957   The sessional allowance was replaced by an annual expense allowance of £750. Although the £1000 salary and the £750 expense allowance were taxable, MPs were allowed to claim as tax free any expenses up to £1,750 incurred in respect of their parliamentary duties.

1964   Following a report by the Lawrence Committee salaries were increased to £3,250.

1965   The Members' Pensions Act was passed introducing a comprehensive scheme for MPs and their families. MPs were to contribute £150 p.a., as would the Exchequer.

1969   A secretarial allowance of £500 was introduced and MPs were allowed free phone calls within the UK.

1972 Salaries were increased to £3,500 following the Boyle Committee Report and the secretarial allowance was doubled to £1,000. A further allowance of £750 p.a. was granted to those MPs living outside London for extra living expenses, while London-based MPs were granted an extra £175 p.a. Travel allowances were extended and a termination grant equal to three months pay was introduced for MPs who lose their seats at elections.

1972 Improved pension scheme was introduced.

1974 Secretarial allowance rose by 75% to £1,750 and the living outside London allowance was raised to £1,050. The London supplement was upped to £228 p.a.

1976 Further improvements in the pension scheme.

1977 Salary increased to £6,270 while secretarial allowances increased to £3,687. London supplement upped to £385, travel allowances further extended and an allowance introduced for overnight stays away from home up to £1,814.

1983 MPs salaries linked to Civil Service rates.

1992 After a Top Salaries Review Board enquiry into office costs MPs voted themselves a substantial increase to nearly £40,000 per annum.

MPs' Pay in Figures

Year	Salary	Office Allowance
1912	400	
1931	360	
1934	380	
1935	400	
1937	600	
1954	1,250	
1964	3,250	
1969	3,250	500
1972	3,500	1,000
1974	4,500	1,750
1975	5,750	3,200
1976	5,750	3,512
1977	6,270	3,687
1978	6,897	4,200

Year	Salary	Office Allowance
1979	9,450	4,600
1980	11,750	8,000
1981	13,950	8,480
1982	14,510	8,820
1983	15,308	11,364
1984	16,106	12,437
1985	16,904	13,211
1986	17,702	20,140
1987	18,500	21,302
1988	22,548	22,588
1989	24,107	24,903
1990	26,701	27,166
1991	28,970	28,986
1992	30,854	39,960
1993	30,854	40,380
1994	31,687	41,308
1995	33,189	42,754
1996	34,085	43,908
1997	43,860	47,568

Ministerial Salaries

	Prime Minister	Cabinet Ministers
1831	5,000	5,000
1937	10,000	5,000
1965	15,250	9,750
1972	23,000	16,000 — E. Health
1978	25,529	17,829
1979	28,765*	24,915
1983	46,660*	37,080
1987	58,650*	47,020
1990	66,851*	55,221
1992	76,234	63,047
1995	80,395	66,489
1996	101,557	86,991
1997	143,860†	103,860†

* Margaret Thatcher opted to take the same salary as other Cabinet Ministers
† Tony Blair and his Cabinet have opted not to draw their full entitlements

MPs Who Have Crossed the Floor of the House This Century*

1996	Peter Thurnham (Bolton NW)	Conservative to LibDem
1996	Alan Howarth (Stratford upon Avon)	Conservative to Labour
1995	Emma Nicholson (Devon West)	Conservative to LibDem
1981	Christopher Brocklebank Fowler (Norfolk NW)	Conservative to SDP
1977	Reg Prentice (Daventry)	Labour to Conservative
1974	Christopher Mayhew (Woolwich East)	Labour to Liberal
1929	W Jowitt (Preston)	Liberal to Labour
1926	J Kenworthy (Hull Central)	Liberal to Labour
1919	J Wedgwood (Newcastle under Lyme)	Liberal to Labour
1918	J Martin (St Pancras E)	Liberal to Labour
1918	E John (East Denbigh)	Liberal to Labour
1915	J Hancock (Mid Derbyshire)	Labour to Liberal
1914	B Kenyon (Chesterfield)	Labour to Liberal
1914	W Johnson (Nuneaton)	Labour to Liberal
1906	A Taylor (East Toxteth)	Conservative to Liberal
1906	J W Walker (Chester le Street)	Liberal to Labour
1904	I Guest (Plymouth)	Conservative to Liberal

* Excludes Labour MPs who defected to the SDP in 1981–2. See list below.

MPs Who Crossed the Floor From Labour to the SDP in 1981–2

Tom Ellis (Wrexham)
R Crawshaw (Liverpool Toxteth)
Tom Bradley (Leicester East)
John Cartwright (Woolwich East)
John Horam (Gateshead West)
Robert Maclennan (Caithness and Sutherland)
J Roper (Farnworth)
David Owen (Plymouth Devonport)

William Rodgers (Stockton)
Neville Sandelson (Hayes and Harlington)
Mike Thomas (Newcastle East)
Ian Wrigglesworth (Thornaby)
E Lyons (Bradford West)
James Wellbeloved (Erith and Crayford)
M O'Halloran (Islington North)
Dick Mabon (Greenock)
R Mitchell (Southampton Itchen)
D Ginsburg (Dewsbury)
J Dunn (Liverpool Kirkdale)
Tom McNally (Stockport South)
E Ogden (Liverpool West Derby)
John Grant (Islington Central)
George Cunningham (Islington South)
R Brown (Hackney South)
J Thomas (Abertillery)
E Hudson-Davies (Caerphilly)
Bruce Douglas-Mann (Mitcham)
B Magee (Leyton)
Bob Mellish (Bermondsey)

Twenty MPs Who Have Voluntarily Resigned Their Seats to Test Public Opinion in a By-election

1986	15 Ulster Unionist MPs	UUP	UUP	14 reelected, 1 lost*
1983	Bruce Douglas-Mann	Lab	SDP	Lost
1973	Dick Taverne	Lab	Dem Lab	Reelected
1955	R Acland	Lab	Ind	Lost
1938	Duchess of Atholl	Con	Ind	Lost
1929	W Jowitt	Lib	Lab	Reelected

*In 1986 all 15 Ulster Unionist MPs resigned their seats in protest at the Anglo–Irish Agreement.

Twelve Husbands and Wives Who Have Served as MPs at the Same Time This Century

1997–	Andrew Mackay and Julie Kirkbride
1997	Alan and Ann Keen
1992–	Gordon and Bridget Prentice
1984–	Peter and Virginia Bottomley
1983–	Nicholas and Anne Winterton
1966–70	J and G Dunwoody
1966–70	R and A Kerr
1945–50	J and F Paton
1938–45	W and J Adamson
1945–60	Aneurin Bevan and Jennie Lee
1929–31	O and C Mosley
1929	H and R Dalton
1928–29	W and H Runciman

Ten Classes of People Who Are Not Allowed to Stand for Election to Parliament

1. Peers of the Realm
2. People convicted of various crimes
3. Bankrupts
4. Priests and Ministers of the Roman Catholic Church
5. Priests and Ministers of the Church of Scotland
6. Priests and Ministers of the Church of England
7. People under the age of 21
8. People with mental disorders
9. Non-British citizens
10. Public servants such as civil servants, judges, police officers and members of the armed forces

MPs Who Have Been Suspended From the House for Defying the Chair

1993	Ian Paisley
1992	Dennis Skinner
1990	Dick Douglas
1990	John Browne
1989	Tam Dalyell
1989	Jim Sillars
1988	Tam Dalyell
1988	Ron Brown
1988	David Nellist
1988	Alex Salmond
1988	Harry Cohen
1988	Ken Livingstone
1988	John Hughes
1987	Daffyd Wigley
1987	Tam Dalyell
1986	Daffyd Wigley
1985	Brian Sedgemore
1984	Martin Flannery
1984	Dennis Skinner
1984	Tam Dalyell
1982	Andrew Faulds
1981	J McQuade, Peter Robinson, Ian Paisley (twice)
1981	Ron Brown (twice)
1972	C Loughlin
1968	Irene Ward
1952	Bessie Braddock
1951	S Silverman
1949	E Smith

Four MPs Who Resigned Their Seats After Being Declared Bankrupt

1903   P McHugh (Nat, North Leitrim)
1909   N Murphy (Nat, S Kilkenny)
1912   H Bottomley (Ind, Hackney South)
1928   C Homan (Con, Ashton under Lyne)

MPs Who Resigned Their Seats Following Censure for Their Conduct in Parliament

1931	T Mardy Jones	Lab, Pontypridd	Abuse of travel voucher
1936	J Thomas	Nat Lab, Derby	Budget leak
1936	A Butt	Con, Balham and Tooting	Budget leak
1947	Gary Allighan	Lab, Gravesend	Contempt of the House after writing in the *World Press News* that MPs gave confidential information to strangers when drunk and took money for tip-offs to the press
1949	J Belcher	Lab, Sowerby	Aftermath of Lynskey tribunal
1963	John Profumo	Con, Stratford on Avon	Lying to the House
1977	John Cordle	Con, Bournemouth East	Poulson affair

Winners of the *Spectator* Backbencher of the Year Award

1984   Nicholas Budgen
1985   James Callaghan
1986   Roy Jenkins
1987   Jonathan Aitken and Richard Shepherd

1988   George Young
1989   Eric Heffer
1990   Tony Benn
1991   Dave Nellist
1992   No winner
1993   Peter Tapsell
1994   Roger Berry
1995   John Redwood
1996   Julian Brazier and Paul Flynn

Winners of the *Spectator* Member to Watch Award

1984	Malcolm Rifkind	1991	David Mellor
1985	Simon Hughes	1992	Michael Forsyth
1986	John MacGregor	1993	Nicholas Soames
1987	Gordon Brown	1994	Peter Mandelson
1988	Tony Blair	1995	Donald Dewar
1989	Charles Kennedy	1996	Menzies Campbell
1990	Brian Wilson		

Winners of the *Spectator* Debater / Questioner / Inquisitor / Campaigner of the Year Award

1984   Jack Cunningham (debater)
1985   Terence Higgins (questioner)
1986   John Gilbert (inquisitor)
1987   No award
1988   Robin Cook (debater)
1989   John Prescott (debater)
1990   Claire Short (campaigner)
1991   Bill Cash (campaigner)
1992   Elizabeth Peacock (campaigner)
1993   Kenneth Clarke (debater)
1994   Edwina Currie (campaigner)
1995   Michael Howard (debater)
        Paddy Ashdown (campaigner)
1996   Robin Cook (debater)

Winners of the *Spectator* Parliamentarian of the Year Award

1984	David Owen
1985	John Biffen
1986	John Smith
1987	Nigel Lawson
1988	Edward Heath
1989	John Smith
1990	Douglas Hurd
1991	Robin Cook
1992	Betty Boothroyd
1993	George Robertson and Geoffrey Hoon
1994	James Molyneaux
1995	Richard Shepherd
1996	Michael Forsyth

Twentieth-century Foreign Secretaries

1997–	Robin Cook	1951–5	Anthony Eden
1995–7	Malcolm Rifkind	1951	Herbert Morrison
1989–5	Douglas Hurd	1945–51	Ernest Bevin
1989	John Major	1940–5	Anthony Eden
1983–8	Geoffrey Howe	1938–40	Viscount Halifax
1982–3	Francis Pym	1935–8	Anthony Eden
1979–82	Lord Carrington	1935	Samuel Hoare
1977–9	David Owen	1931–5	John Simon
1976–7	Anthony Crosland	1931	Marquess of Reading
1974–6	James Callaghan	1929–31	Arthur Henderson
1970–4	Alec Douglas Home	1924–9	Austen Chamberlain
1968–70	Michael Stewart	1924	Ramsay Macdonald
1966–8	George Brown	1919–24	Earl Curzon
1964–6	Patrick Gordon-Walker	1916–19	Arthur Balfour
1963–4	R A Butler	1905–16	Edward Grey
1960–3	Earl of Home	1900–5	Marquess of Lansdowne
1955–60	Selwyn Lloyd	1900	Marquess of Salisbury
1955	Harold Macmillan		

Twentieth-century Chancellors of the Exchequer

1997–	Gordon Brown	1945–7	Hugh Dalton
1993–7	Kenneth Clarke	1943–5	J Anderson
1990–3	Norman Lamont	1940–3	K Wood
1989–90	John Major	1937–40	John Simon
1983–9	Nigel Lawson	1931–7	Neville Chamberlain
1979–83	Geoffrey Howe	1929–31	Philip Snowden
1974–9	Denis Healey	1924–9	Winston Churchill
1970–4	Anthony Barber	1924	Philip Snowden
1970	Ian Macleod	1923–4	Neville Chamberlain
1967–70	Roy Jenkins	1922–3	Stanley Baldwin
1964–7	James Callaghan	1921–2	R Horne
1962–4	Reginald Maudling	1919–21	Austen Chamberlain
1960–2	Selwyn Lloyd	1916–19	Andrew Bonar-Law
1958–60	David Heathcoat-Amory	1915–16	R McKenna
1957–8	Peter Thorneycroft	1908–16	David Lloyd George
1955–7	Harold Macmillan	1905–8	Herbert Asquith
1951–5	R A Butler	1903–5	Austen Chamberlain
1950–1	Hugh Gaitskell	1902–3	C Ritchie
1947–50	Stafford Cripps	1900–2	M Hicks-Beach

Arts Ministers Since 1964

1964	Jennie Lee	1985	Richard Luce
1970	Viscount Eccles	1990	David Mellor
1973	Norman St John Stevas	1990	Tim Renton
1973	Hugh Jenkins	1992*	David Mellor
1976	Lord Donaldson	1992	Peter Brooke
1979	Norman St John Stevas	1995	Virginia Bottomley
1981	Paul Channon	1997	Chris Smith
1983	Lord Gowrie		

* Until 1992 Arts Ministers generally came under the remit of the Cabinet Office. In 1992 the Department for National Heritage was formed. In 1997 its name was changed to the Department of Culture, Media & Sport.

Agriculture Ministers Since 1960

1960	Christopher Soames	1983	Michael Jopling
1964	Fred Peart	1987	John MacGregor
1968	Cledwyn Hughes	1989	John Gummer
1970	James Prior	1993	Gillian Shephard
1972	Joseph Godber	1994	William Waldegrave
1974	Fred Peart	1995	Douglas Hogg
1976	John Silkin	1997	Jack Cunningham
1979	Peter Walker		

Defence Secretaries Since 1962

1962	Peter Thorneycroft	1981	John Nott
1964	Denis Healey	1983	Michael Heseltine
1970	Lord Carrington	1986	George Younger
1974	Ian Gilmour	1989	Tom King
1974	Roy Mason	1992	Malcolm Rifkind
1976	Fred Mulley	1995	Michael Portillo
1979	Francis Pym	1997	George Robertson

Education Secretaries Since 1959

1959	Sir David Eccles	1976	Shirley Williams
1962	Sir Edward Boyle	1979	Mark Carlisle
1964	Quintin Hogg	1981	Sir Keith Joseph
1964	Michael Stewart	1986	Kenneth Baker
1965	Anthony Crosland	1989	John MacGregor
1967	Patrick Gordon Walker	1990	Kenneth Clarke
1968	Edward Short	1992	John Patten
1970	Margaret Thatcher	1994*	Gillian Shephard
1974	Reg Prentice	1997	David Blunkett
1975	Fred Mulley		

* In 1995 the Department of Education was combined with the Department of Employment and became the Department for Education & Employment.

Environment Secretaries Since 1970

1970	Peter Walker	1985	Kenneth Baker
1972	Geoffrey Rippon	1986	Nicholas Ridley
1974	Anthony Crosland	1989	Christopher Patten
1976	Peter Shore	1990	Michael Heseltine
1979	Michael Heseltine	1992	Michael Howard
1983	Tom King	1993	John Gummer
1983	Patrick Jenkin	1997*	John Prescott

* In 1997 the Department of the Environment was combined with the Department of Transport.

Leaders of the House of Commons Since 1945

1945	Herbert Morrison	1972	James Prior
1951	Chuter Ede	1974	Edward Short
1951	Harry Crookshank	1976	Michael Foot
1955	R A Butler	1979	Norman St John Stevas
1961	Iain Macleod	1981	Francis Pym
1963	Selwyn Lloyd	1982	John Biffen
1964	Herbert Bowden	1987	John Wakeham
1966	Richard Crossman	1989	Sir Geoffrey Howe
1968	Fred Peart	1990	John MacGregor
1970	William Whitelaw	1992	Tony Newton
1972	Robert Carr	1997	Ann Taylor

Twentieth-century Home Secretaries

1997–	Jack Straw	1940–5	Herbert Morrison
1993–7	Michael Howard	1939–40	J Anderson
1992–3	Kenneth Clarke	1937–9	Samuel Hoare
1990–2	Kenneth Baker	1935–7	John Simon
1989–90	David Waddington	1932–5	J Gilmour
1985–8	Douglas Hurd	1931–2	Herbert Samuel
1983–5	Leon Brittan	1929–31	J Clynes
1979–83	William Whitelaw	1924–9	W Joynson-Hicks
1976–9	Merlyn Rees	1924	Arthur Henderson
1974–6	Roy Jenkins	1922–4	W Bridgeman
1972–4	Robert Carr	1919–22	E Shortt
1970–2	Reginald Maudling	1916–19	G Cave
1967–70	James Callaghan	1916	Herbert Samuel
1965–7	Roy Jenkins	1915–16	John Simon
1964–5	Frank Soskice	1911–15	R McKenna
1962–4	Henry Brooke	1910–11	Winston Churchill
1957–62	R A Butler	1905–10	H Gladstone
1954-7	Gwilym Lloyd-George	1902–5	A Akers-Douglas
1951–4	David Maxwell-Fyfe	1900–2	C Ritchie
1945–51	Chuter Ede	1900–2	M White-Ridley
1945	D Somervell		

Ten Longest-serving Ministers This Century

29 yrs Winston Churchill (1905–55)
28 yrs Earl of Balfour (1885–1929)
26 yrs R A Butler (1932–64)
24 yrs Duke of Devonshire (1863–1903)
22 yrs Earl of Halsbury (1875–1905)
22 yrs W Long (1886–1921)
22 yrs Austen Chamberlain (1895–1931)
22 yrs Viscount Swinton (1920–57)
21 yrs Marquess of Salisbury (1866–1902)
21 yrs M Hicks-Beach (1868–1902)

Twenty-One Cabinet Ministers Who Suffered Election Defeat While Holding Office

1997	Tony Newton	1965	Patrick Gordon-Walker
1997	Roger Freeman	1964	Anthony Barber
1997	Malcolm Rifkind	1950	A Creech-Jones
1997	Michael Forsyth	1945	Leo Amery
1997	William Waldegrave	1945	Brendan Bracken
1997	Ian Lang	1945	Harold Macmillan
1997	Michael Portillo	1945	John Grigg
1992	Christopher Patten	1945	D Somervell
1979	Shirley Williams	1935	Ramsay MacDonald
1974	Gordon Campbell	1935	Malcolm MacDonald
1970	Jack Diamond		

Twelve Cabinet Ministers Who Died in Office

1916	Lord Kitchener	1940	J Gilmour
1925	Lord Curzon	1943	K Wood
1930	Lord Thomson	1947	E Wilkinson
1931	Viscount Hartshorn	1951	Ernest Bevins
1932	D Maclean	1970	Iain Macleod
1936	G Collins	1977	Anthony Crosland

Ministerial Resignations in the Thatcher and Major Governments

1981	Keith Speed	Defence estimates
1981	Angus Maude	Personal
1982	Nicholas Fairbairn	Handling of a Scottish prosecution
1982	Lord Carrington	Falklands
1982	Richard Luce	Falklands
1982	Humphrey Atkins	Falklands
1982	Nicholas Budgen	Northern Ireland policy
1983	John Nott	Left politics
1983	Cecil Parkinson	Affair with Sara Keays
1985	Ian Gow	Anglo-Irish Agreement
1986	Michael Heseltine	Westland affair
1986	Leon Brittan	Westland affair
1987	Keith Joseph	Personal
1987	Nicholas Edwards	Left politics
1987	Norman Tebbit	Personal
1987	Lord Havers	Personal
1988	Lord Whitelaw	Health
1988	Edwina Currie	Salmonella in eggs
1989	Nigel Lawson	Economic policy
1990	Nicholas Ridley	Remarks about Germany
1990	Geoffrey Howe	Foreign Policy
1992	David Mellor	Affair with Antonia de Sancha
1993	Michael Mates	Links with Asil Nadir
1993	Norman Lamont	Refused to accept demotion
1994	Jonathan Aitken	Resigned to sue the *Guardian*
1994	Tim Yeo	Affair
1994	Earl of Caithness	Private scandal
1994	Michael Brown	Newspaper allegations over gay affair
1994	Neil Hamilton	Links with a lobbying firm
1994	Tim Smith	Links with an accountancy firm
1995	Robert Hughes	Newspaper allegations of extra-marital affair
1996	Steven Norris	Personal reasons
1996	Rod Richards	Newspaper allegations of extra-marital affair

Fifteen Cabinet Ministers Sacked by Margaret Thatcher

Norman St John Stevas	1981	Patrick Jenkin	1985
Mark Carlisle	1981	Peter Rees	1985
Lord Soames	1981	John Biffen	1987
Ian Gilmour	1981	Michael Jopling	1987
Lady Young	1983	Lord Hailsham	1987
Francis Pym	1983	John Moore	1989
Lord Cockfield	1984	Paul Channon	1989
Jim Prior	1984		

Chancellors with the Most Budgets Since 1945

7 Denis Healey (1974–9)
6 R A Butler (1951–5)
6 Nigel Lawson (1983–9)
5 Geoffrey Howe (1979–83)
4 Kenneth Clarke (1993–7)
4 Hugh Dalton (1945–7)
4 James Callaghan (1964–7)
3 Stafford Cripps (1947–50)
3 David Heathcoat-Amory (1958–60)
3 Roy Jenkins (1967–70)
3 Anthony Barber (1970–4)
3 Norman Lamont (1990-3)

Tony Blair's First Cabinet

Prime Minister	Tony Blair
Deputy Prime Minister	John Prescott
Chancellor	Gordon Brown
Foreign Secretary	Robin Cook
Home Secretary	Jack Straw
Lord Chancellor	Lord Irvine of Lairg
Education and Employment	David Blunkett
Leader of the House of Commons	Ann Taylor
President of the Board of Trade	Margaret Beckett
Scotland	Donald Dewar
Wales	Ron Davies
Northern Ireland	Mo Mowlam
Chief Secretary to the Treasury	Alistair Darling
Agriculture	Jack Cunningham
Defence	George Robertson
Health	Frank Dobson
Social Security	Harriet Harman
International Development	Clare Short
Culture, Media and Sport	Chris Smith
Lord Privy Seal	Lord Richard
Chancellor of the Duchy of Lancs	David Clark
Transport	Gavin Strang
Environment	John Prescott
Chief Whip	Nick Brown

William Hague's First Shadow Cabinet

Leader of the Opposition	William Hague
Chancellor	Peter Lilley
Foreign Affairs	Michael Howard
Home Affairs	Brian Mawhinney
Environment and Transport	Norman Fowler
Chairman of the Conservative Party	Lord Parkinson
Education and Employment	Stephen Dorrell
Trade and Industry	John Redwood

Leader of the Commons	Gillian Shephard
Leader of the Lords	Viscount Cranbourne
Defence	George Young
Constitutional Affairs	Michael Ancram
Northern Ireland	Andrew MacKay
Agriculture	David Curry
International Development	Alastair Goodlad
National Heritage	Francis Maude
Chief Secretary to the Treasury	David Heathcoat-Amory
Health	John Maples
Social Security	Iain Duncan-Smith
Chief Whip	James Arbuthnot

Liberal Democrat Spokespeople

Leader	Paddy Ashdown
Deputy Leader	Alan Beith
Chief Whip	Paul Tyler
Leader in the Lords	Lord Jenkins of Hillhead
Agriculture	Charles Kennedy
Education and Employment	Don Foster
Environment	Matthew Taylor
Foreign Affairs	Menzies Campbell
Defence	Mike Hancock
Health	Simon Hughes
Home Affairs	Alan Beith
Local Government	David Rendel
National Heritage	Robert Maclennan
Social Security	Archy Kirkwood
Trade and Industry	Nick Harvey
Transport	David Chidgey
Treasury	Malcolm Bruce
Northern Ireland	Lord Holme of Cheltenham
Scotland	Jim Wallace
Wales	Richard Livsey

Ten Youngest MPs in the House of Commons Today

1973	Clare Ward, Lab	1961	Liam Fox, Con
1973	John Leslie, Lab	1961	David Faber, Con
1967	Graham Brady, Con	1961	William Hague, Con
1963	Matthew Taylor, Lib	1961	Angela Eagle, Lab
1961	Nick Harvey, Lib	1960	Greg Pope, Lab

Eight MPs from Ethnic Minorities

Diane Abbott, Lab	Oona King, Lab
Paul Boateng, Lab	Ashok Kumar, Lab
Bernie Grant, Lab	Mohamed Sarwar, Lab
Piara Khabra, Lab	Keith Vaz, Lab

Ten Places MPs Have Visited on Fact-finding Trips

UNOFFICIAL

1. Paris
2. Washington DC
3. Rio de Janeiro
4. Sydney
5. Tokyo
6. Hong Kong
7. Stockholm
8. Auckland
9. Barbados
10. Jamaica

Ten Places MPs Don't Go on Fact-finding Trips

UNOFFICIAL

1. Skegness
2. Bognor Regis
3. Wigan
4. The Gorbals
5. Isle of Dogs
6. Hartlepool
7. Toxteth
8. Great Yarmouth
9. Rwanda
10. Home

Top Ten Questions Asked on Tours of the Houses of Parliament

UNOFFICIAL

1. Is this building as old as the US of A?
2. Can I crash here?
3. Why do those MPs sit on green leather?
4. Shouldn't they be locked up in a cage?
5. Do we get to meet Mrs Thatcher?
6. How long exactly are two sword lengths?
7. Exactly how early do MPs have an Early Day Motion?
8. Has there ever been a White Rod?
9. Why does the Serjeant at Arms wear stockings, or shouldn't we ask?
10. Hey, where's the sleaze?

Fifty Words and Phrases Ruled Out of Order by the Speaker

Jackal

Tory skunks

Swine

Silly ass

Dirty dog

Stool pigeons

Rat

Jerk

Scoundrel

Snake

Baboons

Political weasel and guttersnipe

Perverter of the truth

Dishonest evasion

Twister

Economical with the truth

Numerological inexactitude

Telling porkies

Seditious blasphemer

Damned lot of cads

Pharisees and hypocrites

Unspeakable blackguard

Stinker

Dunderhead

Smart Alec

Oafish

Lousy

Slippery

Quisling

Right Honourable cheat

Ignorant bigot

Pompous sod

Bollocks

Cretin

Twerp

Boring old twat

Wimp

Bugger all

Bugger

Political shyster

Tweak his goolies

Poached bullshit

Poppycock, bunkum and balderdash

Arrogant little shit

Spiv

Parasite

Mr Oil Slick

Kinnochio

Little squirt

White Livered

Part Two

Elections
and
Voting

Voting in the 1997 General Election

Party	Votes	%	Seats Fought	Seats Won	Lost Deposits
Labour	13,516,632	43.2	639	418	0
Conservative	9,602,857	30.7	648	165	8
Liberal Democrat	5,242,894	16.8	639	46	13
Referendum	811,827	2.6	547	0	505
Scottish National	621,540	2.0	72	6	0
Ulster Unionist	258,349	0.8	16	10	1
SDLP	190,814	0.6	18	3	3
Plaid Cymru	161,030	0.5	40	4	15
Sinn Fein	126,921	0.4	17	2	4
Democratic Unionist	107,348	0.3	9	2	0
UK Independence	106,028	0.3	194	0	193
Green	63,991	0.2	95	0	95
Alliance	62,972	0.2	17	0	6
Socialist Labour	52,110	0.2	64	0	61
Liberal	44,989	0.1	54	0	52
British National	35,833	0.1	57	0	54
Natural Law	30,281	0.1	196	0	196
Speaker	23,969	0.1	1	1	0
Pro Life Alliance	18,545	0.1	53	0	53
UK Unionist	12,817	0.0	1	1	0
Progressive Unionist	10,934	0.0	3	0	0
National Democrat	10,829	0.0	21	0	20
Scottish Socialist Alliance	9,740	0.0	16	0	15
National Front	2,716	0.0	6	0	6
Others	160,631	0.5	300	1	292
Total	**31,286,597**	**100**	**3,723**	**659**	**1,592**

State of the Parties in the House of Commons After the 1997 Election

Labour	419	SDLP	3
Conservative	164	Sinn Fein	2
Liberal Democrats	46	Democratic Unionist Party	2
Ulster Unionists	10	United Kingdom Unionist	1
Scottish National Party	6	Independent	1
Plaid Cymru	4	Speaker	1

Parties Contesting the 1997 Election

All together 169 different labels were used by candidates contesting the 1997 election. Listed below are those who put up two or more candidates throughout the country.

648	Conservative Party
639	Labour Party
639	Liberal Democrats
547	Referendum Party
196	UK Independence Party
159	Natural Law Party
95	Green Party
72	Scottish National Party
64	Socialist Labour Party
54	Liberal Party
57	British National Party
53	Pro Life Alliance
40	Plaid Cymru
29	Rainbow Dream Ticket Party
24	Monster Raving Loony Party
21	National Democrat
20	Socialist Party
18	SDLP
17	Alliance Party

16	Ulster Unionist Party
16	Scottish Socialist Alliance
9	Democratic Unionist
8	Workers Revolutionary Party
6	National Front
5	New Labour
5	Glow Bowling Party
4	Independent Conservative
4	Independent Labour
4	Legalise Cannabis Party
4	Mebyon Kernow
3	Christian Democrat
3	Progressive Unionist
3	Communist Party of Great Britain
3	Socialist Equality Party
2	Communist League
2	Country Field and Shooting Sports
2	Freedom Party
2	Justice Party
2	Loyal Conservative
2	Rizz Party
2	Social Democrat
2	Third Way
2	UK Pensioners Party

Ten Seats with the Highest Turnout at the 1997 Election

1.	Mid Ulster	86.1%
2.	Brecon and Radnorshire	82.2
3.	Stirling	81.8
4.	Wirral South	81.0
5.	Monmouth	80.8
6.	Cardiff North	80.2
7.	Vale of Glamorgan	80.2
8.	North West Leicestershire	80.0
9.	Galloway and Upper Nithsdale	79.7
10.	West Tyrone	79.6

Ten Seats with the Lowest Turnout at the 1997 Election

1.	Liverpool Riverside	51.9%
2.	Hackney North and Stoke Newington	52.2
3.	Manchester Central	52.6
4.	Sheffield Central	53.0
5.	Birmingham Ladywood	54.2
6.	West Bromwich West	54.4
7.	Leeds Central	54.7
8.	Hackney South and Shoreditch	54.7
9.	Kensington and Chelsea	54.7
10.	Vauxhall	55.5

Ten Seats with the Highest Share of the Vote for the Labour Party at the 1997 Election

1.	Bootle	82.9%
2.	Easington	80.2
3.	Blaenau Gwent	79.5
4.	Liverpool Walton	78.4
5.	Knowsley South	77.1
6.	Barnsley Central	77.0
7.	Tyne Bridge	76.8
8.	Merthyr Tydfil and Rhymney	76.7
9.	Houghton and Washington East	76.4
10.	Pontefract and Castleford	75.7

Ten Seats with the Highest Share of the Vote for the Conservative Party at the 1997 Election

1.	Huntingdon	55.3%
2.	Kensington and Chelsea	53.6
3.	Arundel and South Downs	53.1
4.	Sutton Coldfield	52.2
5.	Surrey Heath	51.6

6.	North East Hampshire	50.9
7.	Horsham	50.8
8.	New Forest West	50.6
9.	Chesham and Amersham	50.4
10.	Ruislip Northwood	50.2

Ten Seats with the Highest Share of the Vote for the Liberal Democrats at the 1997 Election

1.	Hazel Grove	54.5%
2.	North Cornwall	53.2
3.	Newbury	52.9
4.	Orkney and Shetland	52.0
5.	Harrogate and Knaresborough	51.5
6.	Sheffield Hallam	51.3
7.	North East Fife	51.2
8.	North Devon	50.7
9.	Cheltenham	49.5
10.	Yeovil	48.7

Ten Seats with the Smallest Share of the Vote for the Labour Party at the 1997 Election

1.	Newbury	5.5%
2.	Christchurch	6.9
3.	Harrogate and Knaresborough	8.7
4.	West Aberdeenshire and Kincardine	9.1
5.	North Cornwall	9.4
6.	South West Surrey	9.4
7.	North Devon	9.8
8.	Cheltenham	10.1
9.	North Dorset	10.2
10.	North East Fife	10.3

Ten Seats with the Smallest Share of the Vote for the Conservative Party at the 1997 Election

1.	Rhondda	3.8%
2.	Glasgow Shettleston	5.5
3.	Glasgow Maryhill	5.9
4.	Glasgow Springburn	6.0
5.	Glasgow Pollok	6.0
6.	Liverpool Walton	6.3
7.	Merthyr Tydfil and Rhymney	6.4
8.	Blaenau Gwent	6.6
9.	Western Isles	6.6
10.	Cynon Valley	6.8

Ten Seats with the Smallest Share of the Vote for the Liberal Democrats at the 1997 Election

1.	Western Isles	3.1%
2.	Glasgow Pollok	3.5
3.	Cumbernauld and Kilsyth	3.8
4.	Glasgow Ballieston	3.8
5.	Ynys Mon	3.8
6.	Glasgow Shettleston	4.0
7.	Kilmarnock and Loudoun	4.0
8.	Dundee East	4.1
9.	Airdrie and Shotts	4.2
10.	Glasgow Springburn	4.3

Ten Seats with the Highest Share of the Vote for the Referendum Party at the 1997 Election

1.	Harwich	9.2%
2.	Folkestone and Hythe	8.0
3.	West Suffolk	7.6
4.	Reigate	7.0

5.	St Ives	6.9
6.	Bexhill and Battle	6.7
7.	Cotswold	6.6
8.	Yeovil	6.6
9.	Falmouth and Cambourne	6.6
10.	Truro and St Austell	6.5

Ten Seats with the Highest Share of the Vote for the UK Independence Party at the 1997 Election

1.	Salisbury	5.7%
2.	Torbay	3.7
3.	Romsey	3.5
4.	Bognor Regis and Littlehampton	3.3
5.	Torridge and West Devon	3.1
6.	New Forest West	3.1
7.	West Dorset	3.0
8.	Arundel and South Downs	2.9
9.	Hexham	2.6
10.	Teignbridge	2.5

Ten Seats with the Highest Share of the Vote for the Socialist Labour Party at the 1997 Election

1.	East Ham	6.8%
2.	Cardiff Central	5.3
3.	Newport East	5.2
4.	Dudley North	4.5
5.	Ealing Southall	3.9
6.	Bradford West	3.4
7.	Birkenhead	3.0
8.	Lewisham Deptford	3.0
9.	Oldham West and Royton	2.9
10.	Barnsley East and Mexborough	2.8

Ten Seats with the Highest Share of the Vote for the Green Party at the 1997 Election

1.	Hackney North and Stoke Newington	4.3%
2.	Islington North	4.2
3.	Stroud	3.9
4.	Tottenham	2.8
5.	Sheffield Central	2.6
6.	Brighton Pavillion	2.6
7.	Louth and Horncastle	2.5
8.	Hornsey and Wood Green	2.4
9.	Birmingham Sparkbrook and Small Heath	2.3
10.	Leeds West	2.2

Ten Seats with the Highest Share of the Vote for the Liberal Party at the 1997 Election

1.	Liverpool West Derby	9.6%
2.	Bethnal Green and Bow	6.6
3.	Slough	3.8
4.	Wolverhampton North East	3.8
5.	Westbury	3.4
6.	Exeter	3.3
7.	Wyre Forest	3.0
8.	Newcastle under Lyme	2.8
9.	Romford	2.6
10.	East Devon	2.6

Ten Seats with the Highest Share of the Vote for the British National Party at the 1997 Election

1.	Bethnal Green and Bow	7.5%
2.	Poplar and Canning Town	7.3
3.	Dewsbury	5.2
4.	West Ham	3.6

5.	East Ham	3.2
6.	Barking	2.7
7.	Dagenham	2.5
8.	Chingford and Woodford Green	2.4
9.	Bradford West	1.8
10.	North Southwark and Bermondsey	1.7

Ten Largest Increases in the Labour Vote at the 1997 Election

1.	Liverpool Wavertree	+23.1%
2.	Crosby	22.4
3.	Brent North	20.4
4.	North East Cambridgeshire	20.2
5.	Hove	20.1
6.	Stockton South	19.7
7.	Wimbledon	19.5
8.	Morecambe and Lunesdale	19.4
9.	Erith and Thamesmead	19.1
10.	Pudsey	19.0

Ten Best Conservative Votes at the 1997 Election

1.	Bethnal Green and Bow	+4.7%
2.	Greenwich and Woolwich	+0.3
3.	Bradford West	-0.8
4.	Linlithgow	-1.2
5.	Liverpool Riverside	-1.3
6.	Liverpool Wavertree	-1.7
7.	Western Isles	-1.8
8.	Glasgow Pollok	-2.1
9.	Glasgow Ballieston	-2.1
10.	Blyth Valley	-2.3

Ten Largest Increases in the Liberal Democrat Vote at the 1997 Election

1.	Sheffield Hallam	+20.6%
2.	Christchurch	19.2
3.	Harrogate and Knaresborough	18.2
4.	Newbury	15.8
5.	Gordon	15.4
6.	Edinburgh West	13.3
7.	Hazel Grove	11.4
8.	Kingston and Surbiton	10.7
9.	South East Cornwall	9.0
10.	Sutton and Cheam	8.5

Ten Largest Decreases in the Labour Vote at the 1997 Election

1.	Bradford West	-11.7%
2.	Bethnal Green and Bow	7.2
3.	Christchurch	5.2
4.	Sheffield Hallam	4.9
5.	Harrogate and Knaresborough	4.8
6.	Cardiff South and Penarth	2.1
7.	Orkney and Shetland	1.6
8.	St Ives	0.8
9.	Airdrie and Shotts	0.7
10.	Newbury	0.6

Ten Largest Decreases in the Conservative Vote at the 1997 Election

1.	Gordon	-21.9%
2.	Woking	20.7
3.	Lewisham West	19.0
4.	Dulwich and West Norwood	18.6
5.	Hastings and Rye	18.4

6.	Dagenham	18.3
7.	Newbury	18.1
8.	Wallasey	18.0
9.	Billericay	17.9
10.	Hayes and Harlington	17.7

Ten Largest Decreases in the Liberal Democrat Vote at the 1997 Election

1.	Greenwich and Woolwich	-22.6%
2.	North East Cambridgeshire	14.6
3.	Bethnal Green and Bow	13.8
4.	Erith and Thamesmead	13.4
5.	Wyre Forest	13.3
6.	Liverpool Wavertree	13.2
7.	Pudsey	12.4
8.	Blyth Valley	11.1
9.	Cotswold	10.4
10.	Stockton South	10.4

Five Largest Labour Majorities at the 1997 Election

1.	Knowsley South	Eddie O'Hara	30,708
2.	Easington	John Cummings	30,012
3.	Bootle	Joe Benton	28,421
4.	Blaenau Gwent	Llew Smith	28,035
5.	Bolsover	Dennis Skinner	27,149

Five Smallest Labour Majorities at the 1997 Election

1.	Wellingborough	Paul Stinchcombe	187
2.	Kettering	Phil Sawford	189
3.	North East Milton Keynes	Brian White	240
4.	Rugby and Kenilworth	Andrew King	495
5.	Romford	Eileen Gordon	649

Five Largest Conservative Majorities at the 1997 Election

1.	Huntingdon	John Major	18,140
2.	Surrey Heath	Nick Hawkins	16,287
3.	East Surrey	Peter Ainsworth	15,093
4.	Sutton Coldfield	Norman Fowler	14,885
5.	Horsham	Francis Maude	14,862

Five Smallest Conservative Majorities at the 1997 Election

1.	South Dorset	Ian Bruce	77
2.	South West Bedfordshire	David Madel	132
3.	Hexham	Peter Atkinson	222
4.	Lichfield	Michael Fabricant	238
5.	Teignbridge	Patrick Nicholls	281

Five Largest Liberal Democrat Majorities at the 1997 Election

1.	North Cornwall	Paul Tyler	13,847
2.	Truro and St Austell	Matthew Taylor	12,501
3.	Hazel Grove	Andrew Stunell	11,814
4.	Yeovil	Paddy Ashdown	11,403
5.	North East Fife	Menzies Campbell	10,356

Five Smallest Liberal Democrat Majorities at the 1997 Election

1.	Winchester	Mark Oaten	2*
2.	Torbay	Adrian Sanders	12
3.	Kingston and Surbiton	Edward Davey	56
4.	Somerton and Frome	David Heath	130
5.	Eastleigh	David Chidgey	754

* At the time of going to press this result was being challenged by the defeated Conservative Candidate, Gerald Malone

Parliamentary Election Results Since 1945

Year	Con	Lab	Lib	Others	Majority	Turnout
1945	213	393	12	22	Lab 146	72.6%
1950	299	315	9	2	Lab 5	84.1%
1951	321	295	6	3	Con 17	82.5%
1955	344	277	6	3	Con 54	76.8%
1959	365	258	6	1	Con 100	78.8%
1964	304	317	9	0	Lab 5	77.1%
1966	253	363	12	2	Lab 96	75.9%
1970	330	287	6	7	Con 30	72.0%
1974 Feb	297	301	14	23	Lab Minority	78.7%
1974 Oct	277	319	13	26	Lab 3	72.8%
1979	339	269	11	16	Con 43	72.0%
1983	397	209	23	21	Con 143	72.7%
1987	376	229	22	23	Con 102	75.3%
1992	336	271	20	24	Con 21	77.7%
1997	165	419	46	29	Lab 179	71.7%

Electorate Figures

	Population	Electorate
1900	41,155,000	6,730,935
1910	44,915,000	7,694,741
1919	44,599,000	21,755,583
1929	46,679,000	28,850,870
1939	47,762,000	32,403,559
1949	50,363,000	34,269,770
1959	52,157,000	35,397,000
1970	55,700,000	39,153,000
1979	55,822,000	41,769,000
1983	56,347,000	43,197,344
1987	56,930,000	43,181,321
1992	57,998,000	43,249,721
1997	58,882,000	44,203,694

Election Turnouts in the Twentieth-century

1900	74.6%	1955	76.7%
1906	82.6%	1959	78.8%
1910	86.6%	1964	77.1%
1918	58.9%	1966	75.8%
1922	71.3%	1970	72%
1923	70.8%	1974 Feb	78.7%
1924	76.6%	1974 Feb	72.8%
1929	76.1%	1979	76%
1931	76.3%	1983	72.7%
1935	71.2%	1987	75.3%
1945	72.7%	1992	77.7%
1950	84%	1997	71.5%
1951	82.5%		

Ten Lowest Votes in General Elections or By-elections

0 votes	F R Lees, Chartists, Ripon in 1860
5 votes	Commander Bill Boaks, Public Safety Democratic Monarchist White Resident, Glasgow Hillhead, 1982
5 votes	Dr Kailish Trevedi, Independent Janata Party, Kensington, July 1988
7 votes	J Connell, Peace Party, Chesterfield, March 1984
8 votes	Esmond Bevan, Independent, Bermondsey, February 1983
10 votes	Peter Reed Smith, Republican, Darlington, March 1983
10 votes	D A Kean, Social Democratic Party, Glasgow Central, June 1980
10 votes	T L Keen, CFMPB, Warrington, July 1981
11 votes	S E Done, ACMFTP, Croydon NW, October 1981
11 votes	H Wise, English Democratic Party, Warrington, July 1981

Ten Seats with the Highest Proportion of Ethnic Minority Voters

1.	Brent South	55.2%
2.	Birmingham Ladywood	53.6%
3.	Birmingham Sparkbrook	52.1%
4.	East Ham	48.5%
5.	Ealing Southall	47.3%
6.	West Ham	43.2%
7.	Brent North	41.5%
8.	Tottenham	38.5%
9.	Bethnal Green and Bow	38.1%
10.	Leicester East	38.0%

Source: *Almanac of British Politics*

Ten Seats with the Highest Proportion of Owner-occupiers

1.	Rayleigh	89.8%
2.	Castle Point	89.4%
3.	Cheadle	87.8%
4.	Charnwood	86.0%
5.	Fareham	85.6%
6.	Solihull	85.4%
7.	Christchurch	85.2%
8.	Old Bexley and Sidcup	85.1%
9.	Ribble Valley	84.9%
10.	Northavon	84.3%

Source: *Almanac of British Politics*

Ten Seats with the Highest Proportion of Council Tenants

1.	Glasgow Baillieston	64.9%
2.	Glasgow Springburn	64.7%
3.	Coatbridge and Chryston	63.8%
4.	Airdrie and Shotts	62.6%
5.	Motherwell and Wishaw	62.0%
6.	Dundee West	61.7%
7.	Southwark North and Bermondsey	61.7%
8.	Glasgow Shettleston	60.4%
9.	Camberwell and Peckham	59.7%
10.	Poplar and Canning Town	59.5%

Source: *Almanac of British Politics*

Ten Highest Conservative Votes in General Elections Since 1929

1.	1992	14,092,891	6.	1955	13,286,569
2.	1987	13,763,066	7.	1970	13,145,123
3.	1959	13,749,830	8.	1983	13,012,315
4.	1951	13,717,538	9.	1950	12,502,567
5.	1979	13,697,690	10.	1964	12,001,396

Ten Lowest Conservative Votes in General Elections Since 1929

1.	1929	8,656,473	6.	1935	11,810,158
2.	1997	9,602,857	7.	1974 Feb	11,868,906
3.	1945	9,988,306	8.	1931	11,978,745
4.	1974 Oct	10,464,817	9.	1964	12,001,396
5.	1966	11,418,433	10.	1950	12,502,567

Ten Highest Labour Votes in General Elections Since 1929

1.	1951	13,948,605	6.	1955	12,215,538
2.	1997	13,516,632	7.	1964	12,205,814
3.	1950	13,266,592	8.	1970	12,179,341
4.	1966	13,064,951	9.	1945	11,995,152
5.	1955	12,404,970	10.	1974 Feb	11,639,243

Ten Lowest Labour Votes in General Elections Since 1929

1.	1931	6,991,000 (inc. National Labour)
2.	1935	8,325,491
3.	1929	8,389,512
4.	1983	8,456,934
5.	1987	10,029,778
6.	1974 Oct	11,457,079
7.	1979	11,532,148
8.	1992	11,559,735
9.	1974 Feb	11,639,243
10.	1945	11,995,152

Highest Liberal Democrat Votes in General Elections Since 1929

1.	1983	7,780,949 (inc. SDP)
2.	1987	7,341,633 (inc. SDP)
3.	1974 Feb	6,063,470
4.	1992	5,999,384
5.	1974 Oct	5,346,754
6.	1929	5,308,510
7.	1997	5,242,894
8.	1979	4,313,811
9.	1923	4,311,147
10.	1922	4,189,527 (inc. National Liberals)

Lowest Liberal Democrat Votes in General Elections Since 1929

1. 1955   722,405
2. 1951   730,556
3. 1935   1,422,116
4. 1959   1,638,571
5. 1970   2,117,035
6. 1945   2,248,226
7. 1931   2,318,510 (inc. National Liberal and Independent Liberal)
8. 1966   2,327,533
9. 1950   2,621,548
10. 1964   3,092,878

Party Share of the Vote in General Elections Since 1918

	Con	Lab	Lib	Other
1918	36	23.7	25.6	14.7
1922	38.2	29.5	29.1	3.2
1923	38.1	30.5	29.6	1.8
1924	48.3	33	17.6	0.8
1929	38.2	37.1	23.4	1
1931	55.2	32.2	10.7	1.9
1935	53.7	38.6	6.4	1.3
1945	39.8	47.8	9	2
1950	43.5	46.1	9.1	1.3
1951	48	48.8	2.5	0.7
1955	49.7	46.4	2.7	1.2
1959	49.4	43.8	5.9	0.9
1964	43.4	44.1	11.2	1.3
1966	41.9	47.9	8.5	1.2
1970	46.4	43.0	7.5	3.2
1974 Feb	37.9	37.1	19.3	5.7
1974 Oct	35.8	39.2	18.3	6.7
1979	43.9	36.9	13.8	5.4
1983	42.4	27.6	25.4	4.7

	Con	Lab	Lib	Other
1987	43.4	31.7	23.2	1.7
1992	42.3	35.2	18.3	4.2
1997	30.7	43.2	16.8	9.3

Ten Most Marginal Labour Seats After the 1992 Election

1. Slough   36
2. Rossendale and Darwen   49
3. Birmingham Yardley   162
4. Ipswich   335
5. Halifax   478
6. Cambridge   580
7. Forest of Dean   732
8. Dudley North   954
9. Swindon North   882
10. Lincoln   964

(All these seats remained Labour at the 1997 election.)

Ten Most Marginal Conservative Seats After the 1992 Election

1. Vale of Glamorgan   19
2. Hayes and Harlington   44
3. Halesowen and Rowley Regis 125
4. Brecon and Radnorshire   130
5. Croydon North   160
6. Stirling   236
7. Portsmouth South   242
8. Corby   342
9. Blackpool South   394
10. Luton South   532

(All these seats fell to Labour at the 1997 election, except Portsmouth South and Brecon and Radnorshire which were lost to the Liberal Democrats.)

Ten Most Marginal Liberal Democrat Seats After the 1992 Election

1. Rochdale   128
2. Inverness, Nairn and Lochaber   736
3. Devon North   793
4. Tweedale, Ettrick and L'dale   1735
5. Cornwall North   1921
6. Cheltenham   1947
7. Bath   2009
8. Argyll and Bute   2622
9. Fife North East   3303
10. Berwick upon Tweed   5043

(All these seats were retained by the Liberal Democrats at the 1997 election apart from Rochdale and Inverness, Nairn and Lochaber which were lost to Labour.)

Labour Party Election Slogans

1997	Britain Deserves Better
1992	It's time to get Britain working again
1987	Britain Will Win
1983	Think positive, act positive and New Hope for Britain
1979	The Labour way is the better way
1974 Oct	Britain Needs a Labour Government
1974 Feb	Let Us Work Together
1970	Now Britain's Strong – Let's Make Her a Great Place to Live In
1966	You *know* Labour Government works and Time for Decision
1964	Let's go with Labour
1959	Britain belongs to you
1955	Forward with Labour
1951	Our First Duty – Peace
1950	Let Us Win Through Together
1945	Let Us Face the Future

Liberal (Democrat) Election slogans

1997	Make the Difference
1992	Changing Britain for Good
1987	The Time Has Come
1983	Working Together for Britain
1979	Real Fight Is for Britain
1974 Oct	Britain Needs a Liberal Government
1974 Feb	No Slogan
1970	What a Life!
1966	For All the People
1964	Think for Yourself!
1959	People count
1955	Crisis Unresolved
1951	The Nation's Task
1950	No Easy Way

Conservative Party Election Slogans

1997	You can only be sure with the Conservatives
1992	The Best Future for Britain
1987	The Next Moves Forward
1983	Challenge of Our Times
1979	Labour Isn't Working and The Right Approach
1974 Oct	Putting Britain First
1974 Feb	Who Governs Britain
1970	A Better Tomorrow
1966	Action not words
1964	Prosperity with a Purpose
1959	Life's better with the Conservatives. Don't let Labour ruin it.
1955	United for Peace and Progress
1951	Britain Strong and Free
1950	This is the Road

Top Twelve Celebrities Who Have Stood for Parliament and Lost

1. Ted Dexter
2. Pamela Stephenson
3. Jonathan King
4. Vanessa Redgrave
5. Eric Morley
6. Ludovic Kennedy
7. Cynthia Payne
8. Auberon Waugh
9. Robin Day
10. A L Rowse
11. William Douglas Home
12. Mark Thomas

Ten MPs Who Won Their Seats with the Lowest Percentage Share of the Vote

1. Russell Johnston	LibDem	Inverness, Nairn and Lochaber	1992	26.5%
2. F J Privett	Con	Portsmouth Central	1922	26.82%
3. J McQuade	DUP	Belfast North	1979	27.61%
4. C W Crook	Con	East Ham	1922	29.74%
5. H G Strauss	Con	Combined Universities	1946	29.98%
6. Rev William McCrea	DUP	Mid Ulster	1983	30.02%
7. M A Bain	SNP	Dunbartonshire East	1974 Oct	31.20%
8. C G Dafis	Plaid Cymru	Ceridigon and Pembroke N	1992	31.29%
9. Peter Robinson	DUP	Belfast East	1939	31.37%
10. J S Holmes	Lab	Derbyshire North East	1918	31.43%

Source: David Boothroyd

Four Occasions When a General Election Has Not Been Held on a Thursday

1931 Tuesday
1924 Wednesday
1922 Wednesday
1918 Saturday

Seventeen By-election Results During the 1992–7 Parliament

May 1993	Newbury	Judith Chaplin	Con	David Rendel	Lib	12.5%	Con–LibDem
July 1993	Christchurch	Robert Adley	Con	Diane Maddock	Lib	11.37%	Con–LibDem
May 1994	Rotherham	James Boyce	Lab	Denis MacShane	Lab	2.77%	Lab–LibDem
June 1994	Barking and Dagenham.	Jo Richardson	Lab	Margaret Hodge	Lab	21.96%	Con–Lab
June 1994	Newham NE	Ron Leighton	Lab	Stephen Timms	Lab	16.30%	Con–Lab
June 1994	Bradford S	Bob Cryer	Lab	G Sutcliffe	Lab	14.12%	Con–Lab
June 1994	Eastleigh	Stephen Milligan	Con	David Chidgey	Lib	21.60%	Con–LibDem
June 1994	Monklands E	John Smith	Lab	Helen Liddell	Lab	19.20%	Lab–SNP
Dec 1994	Dudley West	John Blackburn	Con	Ian Pearson	Lab	29.12%	Con–Lab
Feb 1995	Islwyn	Neil Kinnock*	Lab	J D Touhig	Lab	6.95%	Lab–PC
May 1995	Tayside	Nicholas Fairbairn	Con	Rosanna Cunningham	SNP	11.65	Con–SNP
June 1995	North Down	James Kilfedder	Ind	Robert McCartney	Ind	No swing	
June 1995	Littleborough	Geoffrey Dickens	Con	Chris Davies	Lib	11.70%	Con–LibDem
Feb 1996	Hemsworth	Derek Enright	Lab	J H Trickett	Lab	5.45%	Con–Lab
April 1996	Staffs SE	David Lightbown	Con	B D Jenkins	Lab	22.10%	Con–Lab
Dec 1996	Barnsley East	Terry Patchett	Lab	Jeff Ennis	Lab	3.08%	Con–Lab
Feb 1997	Wirral S	Barry Porter	Con	J K Chapman	Lab	17.24%	Con–Lab

* Neil Kinnock resigned his seat to become a European Commissioner. All other by-elections were caused by the death of the incumbent MP

Ten Signs You're Losing the Election

UNOFFICIAL

1. Even your mother votes for the other guy
2. Suddenly the photo opportunity with the sheep doesn't seem quite so smart
3. Popular campaign chant of 'four more years' refers to your prison sentence
4. Jeremy Paxman describes you on air as 'that total airhead'
5. You hate meeting people
6. Your opponent takes all his party workers to help a nearby marginal seat
7. You are the Conservative candidate in Ebbw Vale
8. You're known as the candidate who can't stop drooling
9. William Hill gives better odds on Camilla marrying Charles
10. Not even your cellmate wants to vote for you – even if he could

Ten Ways to Make Elections More Interesting

UNOFFICIAL

1. Glue up the slot on the ballot box
2. Every time a candidate kisses a baby, have him pelted with eggs
3. Put Peter Snow on Prozac
4. Prime Minister's speechwriter writes a speech of limericks
5. Referendum Party votes to be counted by the same people who count the unemployment statistics
6. Abolish party political broadcasts and replace them with old episodes of *Captain Pugwash*
7. Make the Returning Officers sing the results to the tune of 'Like a Virgin'
8. Ditch the Dimblebores and bring back Robin Day to present election eight programme
9. Abolish postal votes and give out 0891 numbers to raise money for tax cuts
10. Fine opinion poll companies £1 million for every percentage point their predictions are wrong

Ten Excuses for Losing an Election

UNOFFICIAL

1. Should have kept quiet about seeing *Caravaggio* seventeen times
2. Maybe not a good idea to have made that campaign speech in German
3. Misread campaign manager's memo as 'kiss babes' – should have kissed babies
4. Those negative campaign ads about myself were perhaps a mistake
5. That constituency visit by Neil and Christine Hamilton wasn't such a good idea after all
6. Should never have described opponent as a great kisser
7. Couldn't believe they'd be stupid enough to vote for the other guy
8. Shouldn't have accepted that campaign donation from Ian Greer

9. That 'hanging's too good for them' leaflet just wasn't tough enough
10. Thought it was best out of three

Part Three

---

*P*arties
and
*P*olicies

Leaders of the Conservative Party Since 1900

1997–	William Hague	1937–40	Neville Chamberlain
1990–6	John Major	1923–37	Stanley Baldwin
1975–90	Margaret Thatcher	1922–3	Andrew Bonar Law
1965–75	Edward Heath	1921–2	Austen Chamberlain
1963–75	Alec Douglas-Home	1911–21	Andrew Bonar Law
1957–63	Harold Macmillan	1902–11	Arthur Balfour
1955–7	Anthony Eden	1900–2	Marquess of Salisbury
1940–55	Winston Churchill		

Leaders of the Labour Party Since 1900

1994–	Tony Blair	1931–2	Arthur Henderson
1992–4	John Smith	1922–31	Ramsay MacDonald
1983–92	Neil Kinnock	1921–2	J Clynes
1980–3	Michael Foot	1917–21	W Adamson
1976–80	James Callaghan	1914–17	Arthur Henderson
1960–76	Harold Wilson	1911–14	Ramsay MacDonald
1955–60	Hugh Gaitskell	1910–11	G Barnes
1935–55	Clement Attlee	1908–10	Arthur Henderson
1932–5	George Lansbury	1906–8	Keir Hardie

Leaders of the Liberal Party and Liberal Democrats Since 1900

1987–	Paddy Ashdown	1935–45	Archibald Sinclair
1976–87	David Steel	1931–5	Herbert Samuel
1967–76	Jeremy Thorpe	1926–35	David Lloyd George
1956–67	Joe Grimond	1908–26	Herbert Asquith
1945–56	Clement Davies	1900–8	Henry Campbell-Bannerman

Elections for the Leadership of the Conservative Party

1965		Edward Heath 150, Reginald Maudling 133, Enoch Powell 15
1975	*First Round*	Margaret Thatcher 130 Ted Heath 119, Hugh Fraser 16
	Second Round	Margaret Thatcher 110, William Whitelaw 79, Jim Prior 19, Geoffrey Howe 19, John Peyton 11
1989		Margaret Thatcher 314, Anthony Meyer 33
1990	*First Round*	Margaret Thatcher 204, Michael Heseltine 152
	Second Round	John Major 185, Michael Heseltine 131, Douglas Hurd 56
1995		John Major 218, John Redwood 89
1997	*First Round*	Kenneth Clarke 49, William Hague 41, John Redwood 27, Peter Lilley 24, Michael Howard 23
	Second Round	Kenneth Clarke 64, William Hague 62, John Redwood 38
	Third Round	William Hague 92, Kenneth Clarke 70

Elections for the Leadership of the Labour Party

1922		Ramsay MacDonald 61, J Clynes 56
1935	*First Round*	Clement Attlee 58, Herbert Morrison 44, Arthur Greenwood 33
	Second Round	Clement Attlee 88, Herbert Morrison 48
1955		Hugh Gaitskell 157, Aneurin Bevan 57
1960		Hugh Gaitskell 188, Harold Wilson 81
1963	*First Round*	Harold Wilson 115, George Brown 88, James Callaghan 41
	Second Round	Harold Wilson 144, George Brown 137
1976	*First Round*	Michael Foot 90, James Callaghan 84, Roy Jenkins 56, Tony Benn 37, Denis Healey 30, Tony Crosland 17
	Second Round	James Callaghan 141, Michael Foot 133, Denis Healey 38
	Third Round	James Callaghan 176, Michael Foot 137

1980	*First Round*	Denis Healey 112, Michael Foot 83, John Silkin 38, Peter Shore 32
	Second Round	Michael Foot 139, Denis Healey 129
1983		Neil Kinnock 71.2%, Roy Hattersley 19.3%, Eric Heffer 6.3%, Peter Shore 3.1%
1988		Neil Kinnock 88.6%, Tony Benn 11.4%
1992		John Smith 91%, Bryan Gould 9%
1994		Tony Blair 57%, John Prescott 24.1%, Margaret Beckett 18.9%

Elections for the Deputy Leadership of the Labour Party

1952		Herbert Morrison 194, Aneurin Bevan 82
1953		Herbert Morrison 181, Aneurin Bevan 76
1956		J Griffiths 141, Aneurin Bevan 111, Herbert Morrison 40
1960	*First Round*	George Brown 111, F Lee 73, James Callaghan 55
	Second Round	George Brown 146, F Lee 83
1961		George Brown 169, Barbara Castle 56
1962		George Brown 133, Harold Wilson 103
1970		Roy Jenkins 133, Michael Foot 67, Fred Peart 48
1971	*First Round*	Roy Jenkins 140, Michael Foot 96, Tony Benn 46
	Second Round	Roy Jenkins 140, Michael Foot 126
1972	*First Round*	Edward Short 111, Michael Foot 89, Anthony Crosland 61
	Second Round	Edward Short 145, Anthony Crosland 116
1976		Michael Foot 166, Shirley Williams 126
1981	*First Round*	Denis Healey 45.4%, Tony Benn 36.6%, John Silkin 18%
	Second Round	Denis Healey 50.4%, Tony Benn 49.6%
1983		Roy Hattersley 67.3%, Michael Meacher 27.9%, Denzil Davies 3.5%, Gwyneth Dunwoody 1.3%
1988		Roy Hattersley 66.8%, John Prescott 23.7%, Eric Heffer 9.5%
1992		Margaret Beckett 57.3%, John Prescott 28.1%, Bryan Gould 14.6%
1994		John Prescott 56.5%, Margaret Beckett 43.5%

Chairmen of the Conservative Party Since 1970

1997–	Lord Parkinson	1985–7	Norman Tebbit
1995–6	Dr Brian Mawhinney	1983–5	John Selwyn Gummer
1994–5	Jeremy Hanley	1981–3	Cecil Parkinson
1992–4	Norman Fowler	1975–81	Lord Thorneycroft
1990–2	Christopher Patten	1974–5	William Whitelaw
1989–90	Kenneth Baker	1972–4	Lord Carrington
1987–9	Peter Brooke	1970–2	Peter Thomas

Chairmen of the Parliamentary Labour Party Since 1970

1997	Clive Soley	1979	Fred Willey
1992	Doug Hoyle	1974	Cledwyn Hughes
1987	Stan Orme	1974	Ian Mikardo
1983	Jack Dormand	1970	Douglas Houghton

Top Fourteen Donors to the Conservative Party 1995–6

1.	Paul Sykes Group	£214,000
2.	Wittington Investments	£200,000
3.	Hanson	£100,000
4.	Trailfinders	£100,000
5.	P and O	£100,000
6.	Chubb Security	£75,000
7.	Racal	£75,000
8.	Vodaphone	£75,000
9.	Hambros Bank	£56,000
10.	Caledonia Investments	£55,000
11.	Vickers	£55,000
12.	Scottish and Newcastle	£50,000
13.	Sun Alliance	£50,000
14.	Guardian Royal Exchange	£50,000

Source, PIRC and Labour Research

Top Eight Donors to the Labour Party 1995–6

Matthew Harding	£1 million
Political Animal Lobby	£125,000
Capsparo Group	£47,000
GLC	£30,000
Pearson	£25,000
Mirror Group	£21,000
Sun Life	£10,000
Tate and Lyle	£7,500

Source: PIRC and Labour Research

Nine Backbench Groups/Dining Clubs for Tory MPs

Blue Chip Club	One Nation Group
92 Group	Nick's Diner
Lollards	Snakes and Ladders
No Turning Back Group	Dresden Group
Standard Bearers	

Leaders of the Conservative Group in the European Parliament

1994–	Lord Plumb	1979	John Scott-Hopkins
1987	Christopher Prout	1977	Geoffrey Rippon
1982	Henry Plumb	1973	Peter Kirk

Leaders of the Labour Group in the European Parliament

1994	Wayne David	1985	A Lomas
1993	Pauline Green	1979	Barbara Castle
1990	Glyn Ford	1976	John Prescott
1988	Barry Seal	1975	M Stewart
1987	D Martin		

Conservative MPs to Have Been Deselected by Their Constituency Parties Since 1945

1997	Nicholas Scott (Kensington and Chelsea)
1996	David Ashby (Leicestershire North)
	Sir George Gardener (Reigate)
	Michael Stephen (Shoreham)
	Roy Thomason (Bromsgrove)
	Robert Banks (Harrogate)
1992	John Browne (Winchester)
1992	Anthony Meyer (Clwyd NW)
1987	Christopher Murphy (Welwyn Garden City)
1979	R Cooke (Bristol W)
1979	B Drayson (Skipton)
1974 Feb	C Taylor (Eastbourne)
1970	R Harris (Heston and Isleworth)
1964	J Henderson (Glasgow Cathcart)
1964	D Johnson (Carlisle)
1964	O Prior-Palmer (Worthing)
1964	M Lindsay (Solihull)
1959	L Turner (Oxford)
1959	Nigel Nicolson (Bournemouth East)
1954	Lord M Douglas Hamilton (Inverness)
1951	E Gates (Middleton and Prestwich)
1950	G Fox (Henley)
1950	N Bower (Harrow West)
1950	A Marsden (Chertsey)
1945	H Clifton Brown (Newbury)

1945   C Cunningham-Reid (St Marylebone)
1945   J McKie (Galloway)

Seven Most Oddly Named Parties to Have Fought an Election

Belgrano Bloodhunger
Elvisly Yours Elvis Presley Party
Official Acne Party
Blancmange Thrower
Eurobean from the Planet Beanus
Let's Have Another Party Party
Chauvinist Raving Alliance Party

Twelve Minor Parties which have had MPs in the Twentieth-century

Anti Waste League
Campaign for Social Democracy
Common Wealth Party
Communist Party of Great Britain
Co-operative Party
Empire Free Trade Crusade
Independent Labour Party
Independent Parliamentary Group
Irish National Movement
National Democratic and Labour Party
National Party
Scottish Prohibition Party

Nationalisations and Privatisations

1926	Central Electricity Generating Board	Created as Government Body
1926	BBC	Created as Public Corporation
1933	London Passenger Transport Board	Created as Public Sector Body
1943	North of Scotland Hydro-Electricity Board	Created as Public Sector Body
1946	Bank of England	Nationalised
1946	Coal Industry	Nationalised
1946	BOAC and BEA Airlines	Created as Public Sector Corporations
1947	Electricity Industry	Nationalised
1948	Railway Industry	Nationalised
1948	Road Haulage Industry	Nationalised
1948	Inland Waterways	Nationalised
1948	Gas Industry	Nationalised
1949	Iron and Steel Industry	Nationalised
1953	Road Haulage Industry	Privatised
1954	UK Atomic Energy Authority	Created as Public Sector Body
1969	Post Office	Became a Public Corporation
1971	Rolls Royce	Nationalised
1973	Thomas Cook and Carlisle Breweries	Privatised
1975	British Leyland	Nationalised
1976	British National Oil Corporation	Created as Public Corporation
1977	British Aerospace	Created as Public Corporation
1977	British Shipbuilders	Created as Public Corporation
1980	British Aerospace	Privatised
1981	Cable & Wireless	Privatised
1982	Amersham International	Privatised
1982	National Freight Corporation	Privatised
1982	Britoil	Privatised
1982	Associated British Ports	Privatised
1984	Enterprise Oil	Privatised
1984	British Telecom	Privatised
1986	British Gas	Privatised
1987	British Airways	Privatised
1987	Royal Ordnance	Privatised
1987	Rolls Royce	Privatised
1987	British Airports Authority	Privatised

1988	British Steel	Privatised
1988	Rover Group	Privatised
1989	Water Companies	Privatised
1990	Electricity Industry	Privatised
1992-7	Various Trust Ports	Privatised
1995-6	Railway Industry	Privatised
1996	British Energy	Privatised

Labour MPs to Have Been Deselected by Their Constituency Parties since 1987

1997*	Bryan Davies (Oldham Central)
	John Fraser (Lambeth, Norwood)
	Mildred Gordon (Bow and Poplar)
	Max Madden (Bradford West)
	Nigel Spearing (Newham South)
	David Young (Bolton South-East)
	Mike Watson (Glasgow Central)
1992	David Nellist (Coventry South East)
1992	Terry Fields (Liverpool Broad Green)
1992	Sidney Bidwell (Southall)
1992	John Hughes (Coventry North East)
1992	Ron Brown (Leith)
1987	J Forrester (Stoke North)
1987	Ernie Roberts (Islington North)
1987	A Woodall (Hemsworth)
1987	Michael Cocks (Bristol South)
1987	Norman Atkinson (Tottenham)
1987	M Maguire (Makerfield)
1987	Reg Freeson (Brent East)

* Most of these MPs were affected by constituency boundary changes

Post-war Chairmen of the 1922 Committee

1997	Archie Hamilton	1966–70	A Harvey
1992–7	Marcus Fox	1964–66	W Anstruther-Gray
1984–92	Cranley Onslow	1955–64	J Morrison

1972–84	Edward du Cann	1951–55	D Walker-Smith
1970–72	H Legge-Bourke	1945–51	A Gridley

Ten Political Telephone Numbers

0171 930 4433 – Number 10 Downing Street
0171 219 3000 – Houses of Parliament
001 202 456 1414 – The White House
0171 222 9000 – Conservative Central Office
0171 701 1234 – Labour Party Headquarters
0171 222 7999 – Liberal Democrat Headquarters
0131 226 3661 – Scottish National Party
01222 231944 – Plaid Cymru
01232 324601 – Ulster Unionist Party
0171 973 1992 – European Commission (London Office)

A Ten-point Transport Policy for the Next Government

UNOFFICIAL

1. Sedan chairs to be introduced into Central London
2. New ten-man operated buses to be introduced thus curing unemployment at a stroke
3. A fourth London airport to be built at Streatham
4. Everyone over seventy banned from driving a Nissan Sunny
5. Dunkin Donuts to take over all motorway service areas
6. New study to be commissioned on a channel tunnel between England and Scotland
7. All bus lanes to be abolished and turned into Mercedes 500SL lanes
8. Taxi drivers fined £5 for every time they call you 'Guv'
9. Virgin Atlantic flight attendants must prove they are virgins
10. A £200 airport departure tax to be introduced to encourage people to go on holiday in Britain

Ten Things Which Should be Against the Law But Aren't

1. Fraudulent use of a filofax
2. Being drunk in charge of a Labour Party manifesto
3. Smelling of tuna fish
4. Paying for your season ticket at Waterloo station in the rush hour
5. Reading the *Daily Mirror* without just cause
6. Grievous bodily odour
7. Voting without due care and attention
8. Causing a nuisance by asking for extra mayonnaise
9. Wearing a T shirt with 'I ♥ William Hague' on the front
10. The phrase New Labour New Britain

Top Ten Rejected Names for the Liberal Democrats

1. The Liberal Dork-O-Crats
2. The SAS Party
3. The Artist formerly known as the Alliance Party
4. Liberals R Us
5. Literal Demoprats
6. The We'll Put Your Taxes Up Party
7. The Not the SDP Party
8. The Sanctimonious Party
9. The Sad Party
10. The Liberal Party

Part Four

World Politics

Eight Austrian Chancellors Since 1945

1997	Viktor Klima	1961	Alfons Gorbach
1986	Franz Vranitzky	1953	Julius Raab
1983	Fred Sinowatz	1945	Leopold Figl
1970	Bruno Kreisky	1945	Karl Renner
1964	Josef Klaus		

Eleven Belgian Prime Ministers Since 1961

1992	Jean-Luc Dehaene	1973	Edmond Leburton
1981	Wilfried Martens	1968	Gaston Eyskens
1981	Marc Eyskens	1966	Paul Vanden Boeynants
1979	Wilfried Martens	1965	Pierre Harmel
1978	Paul Vanden Boeynants	1961	Theo Lefevre
1974	Leo Tindemans		

Nine Danish Prime Ministers Since 1960

1993	Poul Rasmussen	1971	Jens Otto Krag
1982	Poul Schluter	1968	Hilmar Baunsgard
1975	Anker Jorgensen	1962	Jens Otto Krag
1973	Poul Hartling	1960	Viggo Kampmann
1971	Anker Jorgensen		

Seven French Presidents Since 1947

1995	Jacques Chirac	1959	Charles de Gaulle
1981	François Mitterrand	1954	René Coty
1974	Valéry Giscard D'Estaing	1947	Vincent Auriol
1969	Georges Pompidou		

Sixteen French Prime Ministers Since 1958

1997	Lionel Jospin
1995	Alain Juppé
1993	Edouard Balladur
1991	Edith Cresson
1988	Paul Rocard
1986	Jacques Chirac
1984	Laurent Fabius
1981	Pierre Mauroy
1976	Raymond Barre
1974	Jacques Chirac
1972	Pierre Messmer
1969	Jacques Chaban Delmas
1968	Jacques Maurice Couve de Murville
1962	Georges Pompidou
1959	Michel Debré
1958	Charles de Gaulle

Six German Chancellors Since 1949

1982	Helmut Kohl	1966	Kurt Georg Kiesinger
1974	Helmut Schmidt	1963	Ludwig Erhard
1969	Willy Brandt	1949	Konrad Adenauer

Fifteen Irish Prime Ministers Since 1932

1997	Bertie Aherne	1977	Jack Lynch
1995	John Bruton	1959	Sean Lermass
1992	Albert Reynolds	1957	Eamon de Valera
1987	Charles Haughey	1954	John Costello
1982	Garrett Fitzgerald	1951	Eamon de Valera
1982	Charles Haughey	1948	John Costello
1981	Garrett Fitzgerald	1932	Eamon de Valera
1979	Charles Haughey		

Twenty-Six Italian Prime Ministers Since 1959

1996	Romano Prodi	1978	Francesco Cossiga
1995	Lamberto Dini	1976	Giulio Andreotti
1994	Silvio Berlusconi	1974	Aldo Moro
1993	Carlo Azeglio Ciampi	1973	Mariano Rumor
1992	Giuliano Amato	1872	Guilio Andreotti
1989	Giulio Andreotti	1970	Emilio Colombo
1988	Ciriaco de Mita	1968	Mariano Rumor
1987	Giovanni Goria	1968	Giovanni Leone
1987	Giulio Andreotti	1963	Aldo Moro
1983	Bettino Craxi	1963	Giovanni Leone
1982	Amintore Fanfani	1960	Amintore Fanfani
1981	Giovanni Sadolini	1960	Fernando Tambroni
1980	A Forlani	1959	Antonio Segni

Ten Dutch Prime Ministers Since 1959

1994	Wim Kok	1967	Petrus de Jong
1982	Ruud Lubbers	1966	Jelle Zijlstra
1977	Andreas Van Agt	1965	Joseph Cals
1973	Joop den Uyl	1963	Victor Marijnen
1971	Barend Biesheuvel	1959	John de Quay

Eight Russian and Soviet Heads of Government Since 1922

1991	Boris Yeltsin	1964	Leonid Brezhnev
1985	Mikhail Gorbachev	1953	Nikita Khruschev
1984	Konstantin Chernenko	1953	Georgy Malenkov
1983	Yuri Andropov	1922	Joseph Stalin

Seven Spanish Prime Ministers Since 1939

1995	José María Aznar	1974	Carlos Arias
1982	Felipe González	1973	Luis Carrero
1981	Leopoldo Calvo-Sotelo	1939	Francisco Franco
1976	Adolfo Suárez		

Nine Swedish Prime Ministers Since 1946

1996	Göran Persson	1979	Thorbjorn Falldin
1994	Ingver Carlsson	1978	Ola Ullsten
1991	Carl Bildt	1976	Thorbjorn Falldin
1986	Ingvar Carlsson	1969	Olaf Palme
1982	Olaf Palme	1946	Tage Erlander

Nine Longest-serving World Leaders

Fidel Castro	Cuba	Jan 1959
General Suharto	Indonesia	March 1967
General Gnassingbe Eyadema	Togo	April 1967
El Hadj Omar Bongo	Gabon	December 1967
Colonel Gaddafi	Libya	September 1969
Lt General Hafiz al Asad	Syria	February 1971
France Albert René	Seychelles	June 1977
Hassan Gouled Aptidon	Djibouti	September 1977
Daniel Teroitich Arap Moi	Kenya	October 1978

First Ten Female Presidents and Prime Ministers

Sirimavo Bandaranaike	Ceylon/Sri Lanka	1960–64 and 1970–77
Indira Gandhi	India	1966–84
Golda Meir	Israel	1969–74
Maria Estela Perón	Argentina	1974–75

Elisabeth Domitien	Central African Republic	1975
Margaret Thatcher	United Kingdom	1979–90
Maria de Lurdes Pintasilgo		Portugal
1979		
Vigdis Finnbogadottir	Iceland	1980–
Mary Eugenia Charles	Dominica	1980–95
Gro Harlem Brundtland	Norway	1981 and 1986–89

Twenty-Six Women Politicians Who Have Become Party Leader, Prime Minister or President

Maria Estela Perón (Fmr President of Argentina)
Cheryl Kerno (Leader of the Democratic Party, Australia)
Begum Khaleda Zia (Fmr Prime Minister of Bangladesh)
Sheikh Hasina (Prime Minister of Bangladesh)
Aung San Suu Kyi (Leader of the Opposition, Burma)
Kim Campbell (Fmr Prime Minister of Canada)
Dame Eugenie Charles (Fmr Prime Minister of Dominica)
Edith Cresson (Fmr Prime Minister of France)
Petra Kelly (Fmr Leader of the Green Party, Germany)
Claudette Werleigh (Prime Minister of Haiti)
Vigdis Finnbogadottir (President of Iceland)
Indira Gandhi (Fmr Prime Minister of India)
S Megawatti (Leader of the Opposition, Indonesia)
Mary Robinson (President of Ireland)
Golda Meir (Fmr Prime Minister of Israel)
Helen Clark (Leader of the Labour Party, New Zealand)
Violeta Chamorro (President of Nicaragua)
Gro Harlem Brundtland (Prime Minister of Norway)
Benazir Bhutto (Prime Minister of Pakistan)
Corazón Aquino (Fmr President of the Phillipines)
Hanna Suchocka (Fmr Prime Minister of Poland)
Maria de Lurdes Pintasilgo (Prime Minister of Portugal)
Irene Khamada (Leader of the Republican Party, Russia)
Yekaterina Lakhova (Leader of Women in Russia)
Sirimavo Bandaranaike (Prime Minister of Ceylon/Sri Lanka)

Names of Parliaments Abroad

	Lower House	Upper House
Argentina	House of Deputies	Senate
Australia	House of Representatives	Senate
Austria	Nationalrat	Bundesrat
Belgium	Chamber of Representatives	Senate
Brazil	Chamber of Deputies	Senate
Bulgaria	Sobranje	Grand Sobranje
Canada	House of Commons	Senate
Chile	Chamber of Deputies	Senate
China	National People's Congress	None
Colombia	Chamber of Representatives	Senate
Costa Rica	Legislative Assembly	None
Cyprus	House of Representatives	None
Denmark	Folketing	None
Egypt	National People's Assembly	None
Finland	Diet	None
France	National Assembly	Senate
Germany	Bundestag	Bundesrat
Greece	House of Representatives	None
Hungary	National Assembly	None
Iceland	Althing	Althing
India	Lok Sabha	Rajya Sabha
Indonesia	People's Representative Council	None
Iran	Majlis	None
Iraq	National Assembly	None
Ireland	Dail	Senate
Isle of Man	(Tynwald) House of Keys	Legislative Council
Israel	Knesset	None
Italy	Chamber of Deputies	Senate
Japan	House of Representatives	House of Councillors
Korea, South	National Assembly	None
Latvia	Saeima	None
Liechtenstein	Diet	None
Mexico	Chamber of Deputies	Senate
Netherlands	First Chamber	Second Chamber
Nicaragua	National Assembly	None

Norway	(Storting) Odelsting	Lagting
Pakistan	National Assembly	Senate
Poland	Sejm	Senate
Portugal	National Assembly	None
Romania	Chamber of Deputies	Senate
Russia	Duma	Federation Council
South Africa	National Assembly	Senate
Spain	(Cortes) Congress of Deputies	Senate
Sweden	Riksdag	None
Switzerland	Nationalrat	Staenderat
Syria	People's Council	None
Turkey	National Assembly	Senate
USA	House of Representatives	Senate
Venezuela	Chamber of Deputies	Senate
Zaire	National Legislative Council	None

Top Ten US Presidents

1. Abraham Lincoln
2. George Washington
3. Franklin Roosevelt
4. Theodore Roosevelt
5. Thomas Jefferson
6. Woodrow Wilson
7. Andrew Jackson
8. Harry Truman
9. Dwight Eisenhower
10. James Polk

Source: 1982 *Chicago Tribune* poll of historians and academics

Bottom Ten US Presidents

1. Warren Harding
2. Richard Nixon
3. James Buchanan
4. Franklin Pierce
5. Ulysses Grant
6. Millard Fillmore
7. Andrew Johnson
8. Calvin Coolidge
9. John Tyler
10. Jimmy Carter

Source: 1982 *Chicago Tribune* poll of historians and academics

Eight American Presidents to Die in Office

John Kennedy – assassinated
William Harrison – natural causes
Zachary Taylor – natural causes
Warren Harding – natural causes
Franklin Roosevelt – natural causes
Abraham Lincoln – assassinated
William McKinley – assassinated
James Garfield – assassinated

US Presidents with Most Electoral College Votes

1.	Ronald Reagan	1984	525
2.	Franklin Roosevelt	1936	523
3.	Richard Nixon	1972	520
4.	Ronald Reagan	1980	489
5.	Lyndon Johnson	1964	486
6.	Franklin Roosevelt	1932	472
7.	Dwight Eisenhower	1956	457
8.	Franklin Roosevelt	1940	449
9.	Herbert Hoover	1928	444
10.	Dwight Eisenhower	1952	442

US Presidents with Highest Popular Votes

1.	Ronald Reagan	1984	54.5 million
2.	George Bush	1988	48.9
3.	Bill Clinton	1996	47.4
4.	Richard Nixon	1972	47.2
5.	Bill Clinton	1992	44.9
6.	Ronald Reagan	1980	43.9
7.	Lyndon Johnson	1964	43.1
8.	Jimmy Carter	1976	40.8
9.	Dwight Eisenhower	1956	35.6
10.	John Kennedy	1960	34.2

Oldest US Presidents (at Inauguration)

1.	Ronald Reagan	69	6.	Dwight Eisenhower	62
2.	William Harrison	68	7.	Andrew Jackson	61
3.	James Buchanan	65	8.	John Adams	61
4.	George Bush	64	9.	Gerald Ford	61
5.	Zachary Taylor	64	10.	Harry Truman	60

Youngest US Presidents (at Inauguration)

1.	Theodore Roosevelt	42	6.	Franklin Pierce	48
2.	John Kennedy	43	7.	James Garfield	49
3.	Bill Clinton	46	8.	James Polk	49
4.	Ulysses Grant	46	9.	Millard Fillmore	50
5.	Grover Cleveland	47	10.	John Tyler	51

Eleven Canadian Prime Ministers Since 1935

1993	Jean Chrétien	1968	Pierre Trudeau
1993	Kim Campbell	1963	Lester Pearson
1984	Brian Mulroney	1957	John Diefenbaker
1984	John Turner	1948	Louis St Laurent
1980	Pierre Trudeau	1935	William MacKenzie King
1979	Joe Clark		

Four Chinese Prime Ministers Since 1949

1987	Li Peng
1980	Zhao Ziyang
1976	Hua Guofeng
1949	Zhou Enlai

Ten Indian Prime Ministers Since 1949

1991	PV Narasimha Rao	1979	Charan Singh
1990	Chandra Shekhar	1977	Shri Morarji Ranchodji Desai
1989	Vishwanath Pratap Singh	1966	Indira Gandhi
1984	Rajiv Gandhi	1964	Jal Bahadur Shastri
1980	Indira Gandhi	1947	Jawaharlal Nehru

Thirteen New Zealand Prime Ministers Since 1940

1990	James Bolger	1972	John Marshall
1990	Michael Moore	1960	Keith Holyoake
1989	Geoffrey Palmer	1957	Walter Nash
1984	David Lange	1957	Keith Holyoake
1975	Robert Muldoon	1949	Sidney Holland
1974	Wallace Rowling	1940	Peter Fraser
1972	Norman Kirk		

Twelve Israeli Prime Ministers Since 1948

1996	Benjamin Netanyahu	1984	Yitzhak Rabin
1992	Yitzhak Rabin	1969	Golda Meir
1986	Yitzhak Shamir	1963	Levi Eshkol
1984	Shimon Peres	1955	David Ben-Gurion
1983	Yitzhak Shamir	1953	Moshe Sharett
1977	Menachim Begin	1948	David Ben-Gurion

Fifteen Japanese Prime Ministers Since 1960

1996	Ryutaro Hashimoto	1982	Yasuhiro Nakasone
1994	Tomiichi Murayama	1980	Zenko Suzuki
1994	Tsutomi Hata	1978	Masayoshi Ohira
1993	Morihiro Hosokawa	1976	Takeo Fukuda
1991	Kiichi Miyazawa	1974	Takeo Miki
1989	Toshiki Kaifu	1972	Kakuei Tanaka
1989	Sosuke Uno	1964	Eisaku Sato
1987	Noburu Takeshita	1960	Hayato Ikeda

Eleven Australian Prime Ministers Since 1945

1996	John Howard	1968	John Gorton
1991	Paul Keating	1967	John McEwen
1983	Bob Hawke	1966	Harold Holt
1975	Malcolm Fraser	1949	Robert Menzies
1972	Gough Whitlam	1945	Joseph Chifly
1971	William McMahon		

Last Ten US Presidents

1992	D	Bill Clinton	1968	R	Richard Nixon
1988	R	George Bush	1963	D	Lyndon Johnson
1980	R	Ronald Reagan	1960	D	John Kennedy
1976	D	Jimmy Carter	1952	R	Dwight Eisenhower
1974	R	Gerald Ford	1944	D	Harry Truman

Political Parties in European Countries

Austria
Socialist Party of Austria (SPO) – Left
Austrian People's Party (OVP) – Right
Freedom Party (FPO) – Far Right
The Greens (VGO) – Environmental

Belgium
Christian Social Party (PSC) – Centre Right
Christian People's Party (CVP) – Centre Right
Communist Party (PCB/KPB) – Far Left
Freedom and Progress Party (PLP/PVV) – Right
Flemish Party (Vlammske Blok)– Right
Francophone Democratic Front (FDF)– Centre
People's Union (Volksunie) – Right
Liberal Reform Party (PRL) – Right
National Front (FN) – Far Right

Denmark
Social Democratic Party – Centre Left
Liberal Party – Right
Radical Liberal Party – Right
Conservative People's Party – Right
Socialist People's Party – Left

Finland
Centre Party – Centre Right
Finnish Christian League – Far Right
Finnish People's Democratic League (SKDL) – Left
Finnish Rural Party – Centre
Finnish Social Democratic Party (SDP) – Centre Left
National Coalition Party – Right
Swedish People's Party – Right

France
Centre of Social Democrats – Centre Right
Communist Party (PCF) – Far Left
National Front (FN) – Far Right

Rassemblement pour la République (RPR) – Right
Socialist Party (PS) – Left
Union pour la Démocratie Française (UDF) – Centre

Germany
Christian Democratic Union (CDU) – Centre Right
Christian Social Union (CSU) – Right
Social Democratic Party (SPD) – Centre Left
Free Democratic Party (FDP) – Right
National Democratic Party (NPD) – Far Right
Greens – Environment
Communist Party (KPD) – Far Left
Republican Party – Far Right
Party of Democratic Socialism (PDS) – Far Left

Greece
Pan hellenic Socialist Movement (PASOK) – Left
New Democracy – Right
Communist Party – Far Left
Progessive Party – Right
Ecologist Alternative – Environment
Political Spring – Centre

Hungary
Socialist Workers Party (HSWP) – Far Left
Alliance of Free Democrats (SzDSz) – Right
Independent Smallholders Party (FKgP) – Right
Hungarian Democratic Forum (HDF) – Centre Right
Hungarian Socialist Party (HSP) – Centre Left
Christian Democratic People's Party – Right
Social Democratic Party – Left
League of Young Democrats (FIDESZ) – Right

Ireland
Fianna Fail – Centre Right
Fine Gael – Centre Left
Labour Party – Left
Sinn Fein – Far Left
Progressive Democrats – Right
Green Party – Environment

Italy
Popular Party – Centre Right
Democratic Party of the Left – Far Left
Socialist Party (PSI) – Centre Left
Italian Social Democratic Party – Centre
Republican Party (PRI) – Left
Italian Social Movement National Right (MSI-DN) – Far Right
Forza Italia – Right
Northern League – Right

Netherlands
Christian Democratic Appeal (CDA) – Centre
Labour Party (PvdA) – Left
People's Party for Freedom and Democracy (VVD) – Right
Green Left – Environment

Norway
Labour Party (DNA) – Left
Conservative Party – Right
Centre Party – Centre
Christian Democrat Party – Centre
Liberal Party – Centre

Portugal
Socialist Party (PSP) – Left
Social Democratic Party (PSD) – Centre
Democratic Renewal Party – Centre
Communist Party – Far Left
Centre Democratic Party – Centre
Christian Democratic Party – Right

Spain
Socialist Workers Party (PSOE) – Left
Popular Alliance (AP) – Right
Popular Democratic Party – Centre Right
Communist Party – Far Left
Democratic and Social Centre – Centre Right
Partido Popular (Pd) – Centre Right
National Front (FN) – Far Right

Sweden
Social Democratic Labour Party (SAP) – Centre Left
Communist Left Party (VPK) – Far Left
Centre Party – Centre
Liberal Party – Centre Right
Moderate Party – Right
New Democracy – Right
Green Ecology Party – Environment

Switzerland
Christian Democratic People's Party – Right
Independent Alliance (LdU) – Centre
Radical Democratic Party (FDP) – Centre
Social Democratic Party – (SPS) – Centre Left
Swiss People's Party (SVP) – Right

Turkey
True Path Party – Right
Socialist Democratic Party – Left
Motherland Party – Right
National Democratic Party – Right

United Kingdom
Conservative Party – Centre Right
Labour Party – Centre Left
Liberal Democrats – Centre Left
Scottish National Party – Left
Welsh National Party – Left
Ulster Unionist Party – Right

Political Parties Worldwide

Australia
Australian Labour Party (ALP) – Left
Liberal Party (LP) – Right
National Party (NP) – Right

Canada
Liberal Party – Centre Left
Progressive Conservative Party (PC) – Centre Right
New Democratic Party – Left
Social Credit Party – Left
Reform Party of Canada – Centre
Parti Quebecois – Centre

India
Indian National Congress – Centre Left
Bharatiya Janata Party (BJP) – Right
Communist Party (CPI) – Far Left
People's Party (Lok Dal) – Left
People's Party (Janata Dal) – Centre Left

Japan
Liberal Democratic Party (LDP) – Centre
Japan Socialist Party (JSP) – Left
Democratic Socialist Party – Left
Japan Communist Party (JCP) – Far Left
Clean Government Party – Centre Left

New Zealand
Alliance – Left
ACT New Zealand – Right
New Labour Party – Left
National Party – Right
New Zealand First – Right
New Zealand Labour Party – Centre
New Zealand Self Government – Maori Party

Russia
Agrarian Party – Left
Communist Party – Left
Congress of Russian Communities – Nationalist
Forward Russia! – Right
Liberal Democratic Party – Far Right
Our Home Is Russia (NDR) – Right
Power – Right
Power to the People – Nationalist
Republican Party – Centre Left
Russia's Democratic Choice – Right
Socialist Party of Russia – Left
Women of Russia – Left
Workers' Self Management Party – Right
Yavlinksy-Boldyrev-Lukin Bloc – Centre

South Africa
African National Congress – Left
National Party – Right
Inkatha Freedom Party – Right
Communist Party – Left

United States
Republican Party – Right
Democratic Party – Centre Right
United We Stand – Centre Right

Nine Presidents of the European Union

Walter Hallstein	W. Germany	1958–67
Jean Rey	Belgium	1967–70
Franco Malfatti	Italy	1970–2
Sicco Mansholt	Netherlands	1972–
François-Xavier Ortok	France	1973–6
Roy Jenkins	UK	1977–80
Gaston Thorn	Luxembourg	1981–4
Jacques Delors	France	1985–94
Jacques Santer	Luxembourg	1995–

Top Seventeen International Organisations

	Founding Year	Current Secretary General
Arab League	1945	Esmet Abdel Meguid
Association of South East Asian Nations (ASEAN)	1967	Ajit Singh
Caribbean Community (CARICOM)	1973	Louis Wiltshire
Commonwealth	1931	Emeka Anyaoku
Council of Europe	1949	Catherine Lalumiere
European Union	1951	Jacques Santer
European Free Trade Association (EFTA)	1960	Georg Reisch
North Atlantic Treaty Organisation (NATO)	1949	Javier Solana
Organisation of African Unity	1963	Salim Ahmed Salim
Organisation of American States	1951	Cesar Gavira
Organisation for Economic Cooperation and Development	1960	Jean-Claude Paye
Organisation of the Islamic Conference (OIC)	1971	Hamid Algabid
Organisation of Petroleum Exporting Countries	1960	Dr Subroto
United Nations	1945	Kofi Annan
Western European Union	1955	Willem van Eekelen
World Bank	1946	Lewis Preston

Part Five

General Politics

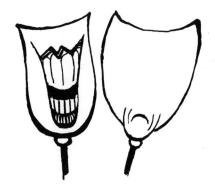

Ten Biggest Trade Unions

1.	Unison	1,369,000 members
2.	Transport and General Workers Union	919,000
3.	GMB	790,000
4.	AEEU	781,000
5.	MSF	482,000
6.	USDAW	283,000
7.	Communication Workers Union	266,000
8.	Graphical, Paper and Media Union	208,000
9.	National Union of Teachers	175,000
10.	Public Services Tax and Commerce Union	165,000

Top Forty Pressure Groups

Age Concern	Promotes rights of the elderly
Aims of Industry	Puts the case for free enterprise and private ownership
Alarm UK	Transport pressure group opposing new road building
Amnesty International	Promotes human rights worldwide
ASH	Anti smoking group
British Field Sports Society	Defends country sports
Bruges Group	Campaigns against moves towards European federalism
Campaign for an Independent Britain	Promotes withdrawal from the EU
Campaign for Freedom of Information	Wants to secure a Freedom of Information Act
Campaign for Homosexual Equality	Campaigns for equal rights for gay men and women
Campaign for Nuclear Disarmament	Campaigns for unilateral and multilateral arms reduction
Charter 88	Argues for constitutional reform including PR

Child Poverty Action Group	Promotes action for the relief of poverty among children
Compassion in World Farming	Campaigns for improvements in animal welfare
Council for the Protection of Rural England	Encourages protection of the countryside
Country Landowners Association	Promotes interests of rural landowners
Cyclists Public Affairs Group	Lobbying group formed to promote rights of cyclists
Electoral Reform Society	Campaigns for proportional representation
Federal Trust	Promotes the idea of a federal Europe
FOREST	Freedom Organisation for the Right to Enjoy Smoking Tobacco
Freedom Association	Campaigns for freedom and free enterprise
Friends of the Earth	Promotes environmentally friendly policies
Howard League for Penal Reform	Promotes fair treatment for prisoners and penal reform
Inland Waterways Association	Campaigns for upgrading of Britain's waterways
League Against Cruel Sports	Campaigns against fox hunting and for animal welfare
Liberty	Campaigns to extend civil liberties and human rights
NACRO	Campaigns for the care and resettlement of offenders
National Consumer Council	Promotes consumer rights
National Farmers' Union	Promotes farming interests
National Viewers and Listeners Association	Campaigns against pornography and obscenity on TV
NSPCC	Campaigns for children
Ramblers' Association	Defends rights of the public to roam the countryside
RSPB	Campaigns for birds and their environment
RSPCA	Promotes rights of animals
Society for the Protection of Unborn Children	Campaigns to end legalised abortion

Stonewall	Promotes equal rights for gays and lesbians
Terrence Higgins Group	Promotes rights of people suffering from AIDS and HIV
300 Group	Promotes equal representation for women in Parliament
Tidy Britain Group	Campaigns for a litter-free environment
Transport 2000	Campaigns for a sustainable transport policy

Top Fifteen Policy Think Tanks

Action Centre for Europe   1995   Centre/Right

Pro-Europe, pro-business think tank run by former Tory MEP Michael Welsh

Adam Smith Institute   1977   Right

Promotes free market economics and the beliefs of Adam Smith. Run by economics guru Madsen Pirie.

Centre for Policy Studies   1974   Right

Formed by Margaret Thatcher and Sir Keith Joseph, promotes case for limited government, privatisation and social stability. Heyday in the 1980s, still very influential. Run by formidable former Ken Clarke adviser Tessa Keswick

Demos   1993   Centre/Left

Seeks to promote long-term political policy-thinking. Specialises in producing thought-provoking New Labourish philosophy papers. Led by Geoff Mulgan, now part of Tony Blair's Policy Unit. Increasingly influential on the Left.

European Foundation   1995   Right

Front organisation for Euro-sceptic MP Bill Cash. Promotes free trade within the EU and a widening of EU membership without a federal union. Run by one-time Thatcher biographer and *Daily Mail* hack Russell Lewis.

European Movement   1948   Centre

Seeks to promote understanding of the EU and the idea of European federal union. Chaired by former Tory MP Hugh Dykes.

European Policy Forum   1992   Centre/Right

Breakaway from the Institute of Economic Affairs led by Graham Mather, now also a Tory MEP. Seeks to promote decentralised market-led solutions to policy problems in Britain and Europe.

Fabian Society   1884   Left

Left-leaning talking-shop now metamorphosising into a think tank. Populist research papers widely taken notice of on the Left. Former director Stephen Twigg now Labour MP for Edmonton.

Institute for Fiscal Studies   1969   Centre

Interprets tax and fiscal policy. Its economic research papers are highly thought of. Led by the media-friendly Andrew Dilnot.

Institute for Public Policy Research   1989   Left

The most influential Left-leaning think tank in the early 1990s. Now competing with Demos. Formed by former Kinnock adviser Patricia Hewitt, now a Labour MP. Sought to provide an alternative to the free market think tanks of the Right.

Institute of Economic Affairs   1957   Right

Seeks to improve public understanding of free market economics and principles. Achieved a high profile in the late 1970s under the leadership of Ralph (now Lord) Harris and then Graham Mather. Now led by John Blundell. Produces widely read papers with great regularity. Like the Centre for Policy Studies and Adam Smith Institute, noted for proposing radical ideas considered bizarre at the time but then adopted as government policy a few years later.

Politeia   1995   Right

Breakaway from the Centre for Policy Studies by former CPS deputy director Dr Sheila Lawlor. Counts Cecil Parkinson and Lord Cranbourne as patrons. Deals mostly with social and education policy.

Royal Institute of International Affairs   1920   Centre

Seeks to promote understanding of international affairs. Very Establishment, very professional, very rich.

Social Affairs Unit   1980 Right

Promotes education and research into social and economic affairs. Run by Digby Anderson, its profile is rising as is the frequency of its publications.

Social Market Foundation   1989 Centre/Right

Stands for the market system in all areas of public policy. Former CPS Director (now Tory MP) David Willetts was its first director and its patron is Lord Skidelsky. Has had difficulty in defining itself on the Right but has produced thought-provoking policy papers on regulation and market issues.

Tip O'Neill's Checklist for Successful Politicians

1. It's a round world – what goes around comes around.
2. You can accomplish anything if you're willing to let someone else take the credit.
3. Never lose your idealism.
4. Lead by consent not by demand.
5. You can switch a position but do it quickly and openly.
6. Learn to say 'I don't know but I will find out'.
7. KISS – Keep it simple and stupid.
8. Never speak of yourself in the third person.
9. Tell the truth the whole time and then you don't have to remember what you said.
10. No chore is too small.

Colin Powell's Rules of Life

1. It ain't as bad as you think. It will look better in the morning.
2. Get mad. Then get over it.
3. Avoid having your ego so close to your position that when your position falls, your ego goes with it.
4. It can be done!
5. Be careful what you choose. You may get it.
6. Don't let adverse facts stand in the way of a good decision.
7. You can't make someone else's choices. You shouldn't let someone else make yours.
8. Check small things.
9. Share credit.
10. Remain calm. Be kind.
11. Have a vision. Be demanding.
12. Don't take counsel of your fears or naysayers.
13. Perpetual optimism is a force multiplier.

Source: *My American Journey* by Colin Powell.

Key Dates in Twentieth-Century British Political History

1997   Labour Party wins biggest landslide in modern political history
1992   Maastricht Treaty ratified
1989   House of Commons is televised
1982   Parliament votes to repatriate Canada's constitution
1979   Margaret Thatcher becomes first woman Prime Minister
1975   Referendum on EEC Membership
1973   Britain enters EEC
1972   Secret ballots introduced in UK elections
1971   Ban on reporting of parliamentary proceedings lifted
1970   Eighteen year olds allowed to vote
1958   Women allowed to sit in the House Lords
1929   Margaret Bonfield becomes first woman Cabinet Minister
1928   Voting age for women reduced to twenty-one
1918   Women allowed to vote for the first time
1911   Parliament Act limits rights of House of Lords to veto legislation

Top Twenty Political 'Isms'

Absolutism	Maoism
Anarchism	Nihilism
Communism	Pacifism
Entryism	Paternalism
Fascism	Racism
Feminism	Sexism
Federalism	Socialism
Gaullism	Stalinism
Libertarianism	Thatcherism
Marxism-Leninism	Trotskyism

Thirty Political Acronyms

ACAS – Arbitration and Conciliation Advisory Service

CHOGM – Commonwealth Heads of Government Meeting

COREPER – Committee of Permanent Representatives at the European Commission

ECOFIN – EU Council of Economics and Finance Ministers

ECOSOC – EU Economic and Social Committee

ECU – European Currency Unit

EDM – Early Day Motion

EFTA – European Free Trade Association

EMU – European Monetary Union

FCO – Foreign and Commonwealth Office

G7 – Group of Seven

GATT – General Agreement on Tariffs and Trade

GDP – Gross Domestic Product

IGC – Inter Governmental Conference

ILO – International Labour Organisation

IPPR – Institute for Public Policy Research

NATO – North Atlantic Treaty Organisation

NEC – National Executive Committee of the Labour Party

NEDC – National Economic Development Council

OPEC – Organisation of Petroleum Exporting Countries

PLP – Parliamentary Labour Party

PSBR – Public Sector Borrowing Requirement
QUANGO – Quasi Autonomous Non Governmental Organisation
SDI – Strategic Defense Initiative
SDLP – Social Democratic and Labour Party
SEATO – South East Asia Treaty Organisation
SHAPE – Supreme Headquarters Allied Powers Europe
TINA – There Is No Alternative
UDA – Ulster Defence Association
UNESCO – United Nations Educational, Scientific and Cultural Organisation

Top Ten Lobbying Companies

APCO – Founded in April 1995 by Greer renegades Simon Milton, Angie Bray and John Fraser. Part of the Grey Communications Group, APCO has grown rapidly to be one of the biggest lobby companies in Westminster.

Decision Makers – Run by the formidable Maureen Tomison, DM (as it is now called) hit the headlines over its relationship with Dame Angela Rumbold.

GCI London – Formed in 1991 after the merger of GCI Sterling and McAvoy Bayley.

GJW Government Relations – Formed in 1980 by former Commons researchers Andrew Gifford, Jenny Jeger and Wilf Weeks. Currently the biggest and one of the best lobby companies. Recently moved to new offices close to Parliament.

GPC Connect – Established in 1986 as Countrywide Political Communications, merged with Connect Public Affairs in mid-1990s and is one of the few consultancies to specialise in particular policy areas. Headed by Angela Casey, Martin Smith and Julia Harrison.

Lowe Bell Political – Part of Tim Bell's PR group, headed by former Number Ten adviser Stephen Sherbourne and former Westminster strategy director Kevin Bell. Lady Thatcher's press officer, Elizabeth Buchanan, is also on the staff of Britain's most pricey lobby outfit.

Market Access – Established in 1984 by David Boddy, who remains chairman, the company is now headed up by former Prescott staffer Mike Craven. Rivals GJW as biggest and best.

Public Policy Unit – Formed in 1985 by former Greer man Charles Miller. Miller now acts as secretary to the lobbyists trade association, the Association of Professional Political Consultants.

Westminster Communications – Founded in 1968 and with Ian Greer Associates benefited from the mid-1980s boom in lobbying activity. Headed by Richard Faulkner, it has a predominantly public-sector client base.

Westminster Strategy – Founded in 1986, it rapidly grew to rival GJW as the biggest lobby firm in Westminster. Michael Burrell is the front man with former Blunkett staffer Mike Lee as number two.

Thirteen British Political Web Sites on the Internet

Alliance Party of Northern Ireland	http://www.unite.net/customers/alliance/
British National Party	http://ngwwmall.com/frontier/bnp/
Central Office of Information	http://www.coi.gov.uk/coi/
Conservative Party	http://www.conservative-party.org.uk
HM Treasury	http://www.hm-treasury.gov.uk
Labour Party	http://www.poptel.org.uk/labour-party/
Liberal Democrats	http://www.libdems.org.uk
Natural Law Party	http://www.u-net.com/~wrcs/nlp/home.htm
Plaid Cymru	http://www.wales.com/political-party/plaid-cymru
Referendum Party	http://www.demon.co.uk/dita/europe/rp/
Scottish National Party	http://www.rmplc.co.uk/eduweb/sites/hamish/snp.html
Trades Unions Congress	http://www.tuc.org.uk
Ulster Unionist Party	http://www.gpl.net/customers/uup/

Top Ten Political Academics

1.	David Butler	Oxford University
2.	Anthony King	University of Essex
3.	Ivor Crewe	University of Essex

4.	Dennis Kavanagh	University of Liverpool
5.	Philip Norton	Hull University
6.	Richard Rose	Strathclyde University
7.	Michael Thrasher	Plymouth University
8.	Tony Travers	London School of Economics
9.	Alan Doig	University of Liverpool
10.	Patrick Dunleavy	London School of Economics

Top Ten Post-war Best Prime Ministers We Never Had

UNOFFICIAL

1. R A Butler
2. Denis Healey
3. Michael Heseltine
4. John Smith
5. David Owen
6. Hugh Gaitskell
7. Aneurin Bevan
8. Joe Grimond
9. Tony Benn
10. Enoch Powell

Part Six

Quotations

Top Ten Conservative Quotes

A Conservative is a man who sits and thinks – mostly sits.

Woodrow Wilson

To be a Conservative is to prefer the tried to the untried, the fact to mystery, the actual to the possible, the limited to the unbounded, the near to the distant, the sufficient to the super-abundant, the convenient to the perfect present, laughter to utopian bliss.

Michael Oakshott

The Conservatives conserve what you've got, the Liberals are liberal with it and Labour gives it all away.

Ted Hunt

Of course, nobody likes the Conservatives. They only vote for us because they think we are right.

Peter Lilley

In the Conservative Party we have no truck with outmoded Marxist doctrine about class warfare. For us it is not who you are, who your family is or where you come from that matters, but what you are and what you can do for your country that counts.

Margaret Thatcher

A liberal conservative is a man who thinks things ought to progress but would rather they remained as they are.

Fitzjames Stephens

A Conservative Government is an organised hypocrisy.

Benjamin Disraeli

What is conservatism? Is it not adherence to the old and tried, against the new and the untried?

Abraham Lincoln

There is always a certain meanness in the argument of conservatism, joined with a certain superiority in its fact.

Ralph Waldo Emerson

Nothings commends a radical change to an Englishman more than the belief that it is really conservative.

H A L Fisher

Top Ten Socialist Quotes

An extreme Socialist is one who wants to abolish public schools tomorrow. A moderate Socialist wants to abolish them after his children have finished going there.

Norman Tebbit

I sometimes think the Labour Party is like a pub where the mild is running out. If someone does not do something soon, all that is left will be bitter and all that is bitter will be left.

Margaret Thatcher

As with the Christian religion, the worst advert for Socialism is its adherents.

George Orwell

I haven't read Karl Marx. I got stuck on the footnote on page two.

Harold Wilson

Socialism is nothing but the capitalism of the lower classes.

Oswald Spengler

As far as Socialism means anything, it must be about the wider distribution of smoked salmon and caviar.

Richard Marsh

The term 'democratic socialist' makes as much sense as 'pregnant virginity'.

Russell Prowse, Australian industrialist

Democracy and socialism are means to an end, not the end itself.

Jawaharlal Nehru

The typical Socialist is . . . a prim little man with a white collar job, usually a secret teetotaller and often with vegetarian leanings, with a history of Nonconformity behind him, and, above all, with a social position which he has no intention of forfeiting.

George Orwell

Socialism is what a Labour Government does.

Herbert Morrison

Top Ten Liberal Quotes

We all know what happens to people who stay in the middle of the road. They get run over.

Aneurin Bevan

The trouble with many Liberals is that they talk a lot of cock.

Cyril Smith

Liberal – worshipper of power without power.

George Orwell

If God had been a Liberal there would not have been ten commandments, there would have been ten suggestions.

Malcolm Bradbury

The closest thing to a Tory in disguise is a Whig in power.

Benjamin Disraeli

A Liberal is a man who leaves a room before the fight begins.

Heywood Broun

A Liberal is a man too broadminded to take his own side in a quarrel.

Robert Frost

I have the good fortune to be the first Liberal leader for half a century who is able to say at the end of our general assembly: go back to your constituencies and prepare for government.

David Steel in 1981

A Radical is a man with both feet firmly planted – in the air. A Conservative is a man with two perfectly good legs who, however, has never learned to walk forward. A Reactionary is a somnambulist walking backwards. A Liberal is a man who uses his legs and his hands at the behest – at the command of his head.

Franklin D Roosevelt

Testators would do well to provide some indication of the particular Liberal Party which they have in mind, such as a telephone number or a Christian name.

A P Herbert

Top Ten Quotes on Political Power

Whenever a man has cast a longing eye on offices, a rottenness begins in his conduct.

Thomas Jefferson

I have no ambition to govern men. It is a painful and thankless office.

Thomas Jefferson

Anyone who deliberately tries to get himself elected to a public office is permanently disqualified from holding one.

Thomas More

Political power grows out of the barrel of a gun.

Mao Tse Tung

Unlimited power is apt to corrupt the minds of those who possess it; and this I know, my Lords, that where law ends, tyranny begins.

William Pitt

The depository of power is always unpopular.

Benjamin Disraeli

Power corrupts, but absolute power corrupts absolutely.

Adlai Stevenson

Nearly all men can stand adversity, but if you want to test a man's character give him power.

Abraham Lincoln

I have an enormous personal ambition. I want to shift the entire planet. And I'm doing it. I am a famous person. I represent real power.

Newt Gingrich

Political power, properly so called, is merely the organised power of one class for oppressing another.

Karl Marx

Top Ten Quotes on the Commons and Lords

The Commons must bray like asses every day to appease their electoral hordes.

A P Herbert

If only the House of Commons had emulated the Lords' admirable inactivity, we should have been saved from a great many foolish acts.

Lambert Jeffries

But then the prospect of a lot of dull MPs in close proximity, all thinking for themselves, is what no man can face with equanimity.

W S Gilbert

The cure for admiring the House of Lords is to go and look at it.

Walter Bagehot

I don't go to the House of Lords any more. I went once but my umbrella was stolen by a Bishop.

Lord Berners

The British House of Lords is the British Outer Mongolia for retired politicians.

Tony Benn

The House of Commons is absolute. It is the State. *L'Etat c'est moi.*

Benjamin Disraeli (Coningsby, 1844)

There is no more striking illustration of the immobility of British institutions than the House of Commons.

Herbert Asquith

The House of Lords, an illusion to which I have never been able to subscribe – responsibility without power, the prerogative of the eunuch throughout the ages.

Tom Stoppard

The House of Lords is a perfect eventide home.

Baroness Stocks

Those who would enjoy the pleasures of democracy, said the doctor, must school themselves to suffer the law's delay.

Ivor Brown

Democracy means government by discussion, but it is only effective if you can stop people talking.

Clement Attlee

Democracy is the process by which people choose the man who will get the blame.

Bertrand Russell

A People's Republic is a place where you do what you are told or get shot. National Liberation Movements are organisations that are trying to create People's Republics.

Thomas Sowell

A democracy is a government in the hands of low birth, no property and vulgar employments.

Aristotle

The disadvantage of free elections is that you can never be sure who is going to win them.

Molotov

The world is weary of statesmen whom democracy has degraded into politicians.

Benjamin Disraeli

Democracy means simply the bludgeoning of the people, by the people, for the people.

Oscar Wilde

Without democracy Socialism would be worth nothing, but democracy is worth a great deal even when it is not Socialist.

A J P Taylor

Under democracy one party always devotes its chief energies to prove that the other party is unfit to rule – and both commonly succeed, and they are right.

H L Mencken

Top Ten Quotes on Economics

There are two problems in my life. The political ones are insoluble and the economic ones are incomprehensible.

Alec Douglas-Home

Private greed is making money selling people what they want. Public service is failing to sell them what they don't want.

Thomas Sowell

One man's wage increase is another man's price increase.

Harold Wilson

It's a recession when your neighbour loses his job. It's a depression when you lose your own.

Harry Truman

Good news is, a bus full of supply-siders went over the cliff. Bad news is, there were three empty seats.

Bob Dole

Compassion is the use of tax money to buy votes. Insensitivity is the objection to the use of tax money to buy votes.

Thomas Sowell

Balancing your budget is like protecting your virtue – you have to learn when to say no.

Ronald Reagan

Balancing the budget is like going to heaven. Everybody wants to do it but nobody wants to make the trip.

Phil Gramm

Politically there is no record of the continuance of political freedoms when economic freedoms have died.

Rhodes Boyson

Economics are the method; the object is to change the soul.

Margaret Thatcher

Reorganising the civil service is like drawing a knife through a bowl of marbles.

Government is about principles. And the principle is, never act on principle.

Central government must not interfere with the right of freely elected local councils to pour ratepayers' money down the drain.

A good political speech is not one in which you can prove that the man is telling the truth; it is one where no one else can tell he is lying.

If the Prime Minister is told something personally, even if he doesn't know it officially, he can use his personal knowledge to start official inquiries to get official confirmation of personal suspicions so that what he originally knew personally but not officially he will then know officially as well as personally.

Turning a blind eye to corruption could never be government policy. It is merely government practice.

Any statement in a politician's memoirs can represent one of six levels of reality – what happened, what he believed happened, what he would have like to have happened, what he wants to believe happened, what he wants other people to believe happened, what he wants other people to believe he believe happened.

Stalling Ministers: the five stage approach. 1 – The administration is in its early months and there's an awful lot to do at once. 2 – Something ought to be done but is this the right way to achieve it? 3 – The idea is good but the time is not ripe. 4 – The proposal has run into technical, logistical and legal difficulties which are being sorted out. 5 – Never refer to the matter or reply to the Minister's notes. By the time he taxes you with it face to face you should be able to say it looks unlikely if anything can be done until after the election.

Irregular verb: I have an independent mind, you are an eccentric, he is round the twist.

Being an MP is a vast subsidised ego-trip. It's a job that needs no qual-ifications, it has no compulsory hours of work, no performance stan-dards and provides a warm room, a telephone and subsidised meals to a bunch of self-important windbags and busybodies who suddenly find themselves being taken seriously because they've got the letters 'MP' after their name.

Top Ten Political Insults

When they circumcised Herbert Samuel they threw away the wrong bit.

David Lloyd George, Prime Minister 1916–21

The Liberals are a beanbag kind of a party that looks like the last person who sat in it.

Bob Rae, former Premier of Ontario

Suppose you were an idiot. And suppose you were a member of Congress. But I repeat myself.

Mark Twain, author

The Right Honourable Gentleman's smile is like the fittings on a coffin.

Benjamin Disraeli to Sir Robert Peel

My views of him [Newt Gingrich] are somewhat similar to those of a fire hydrant toward a dog.

Jim Wright, former Speaker of the US House of Representatives

Mr Benn is a kind of perennial youth who immatures with age.

Harold Wilson

In any civilised country Heath would have been left hanging upside down from a petrol pump years ago.

Auberon Waugh

Jerry's the only man I ever knew who can't fart and chew gum at the same time.

Lyndon Johnson, of Gerald Ford

I wouldn't piss down Jerry Brown's throat if his heart was on fire.

James Carville, Adviser to Bill Clinton

Arthur Scargill possesses the remarkable ability to blush when telling the truth.

David Hunt OBE MP, Former Cabinet Minister

Top Ten Memorable One-liners from Margaret Thatcher

It will be years, and not in my time, before a woman will lead the Party or become Prime Minister.

1974

No! No! No!

Opposing proposals put forward by Jacques Delors, 1990

Just rejoice, rejoice!

To reporters after the recapture of South Georgia

The lady's not for turning.

At the 1981 Conservative Party Conference

Every Prime Minister needs a Willie.

On her deputy, Willie Whitelaw

Being in power is like being a lady – if you have to tell people you are, you aren't.

One of us.

Describing political allies

Where there is discord may we bring harmony.

Quoting St Francis of Assisi, May 1979

We have become a Grandmother.

I fight on, I fight to win.

Leadership election, 1990

Top Ten Quotes on the Art of Politics

Politics is show business for ugly people.

Paul Begala, adviser to Bill Clinton

The art of politics is learning to walk with your back to the wall, your elbows high and a smile on your face.

Jean Chrétien, Canadian Prime Minister

Sex is like politics. You don't have to be good at it to enjoy it.

Barrie Goldwater, former US Senator

Politics is not the art of the possible. It consists in choosing between the disastrous and the unpalatable.

J K Galbraith

Politics is just like show business. You have a hell of an opening, you coast for a while, you have a hell of a closing.

Ronald Reagan

A politician is an animal who can sit on the fence and keep both ears to the ground.

H L Mencken

A politician is a person with whose politics you do not agree. If you agree with him he is a Statesman.

David Lloyd George

If you see a snake, kill it. Don't appoint a committee on snakes.

Ross Perot

As a politician never believes what he says, he is surprised when others believe him.

Charles de Gaulle

There is no act of treachery or meanness of which a political party is not capable, for in politics there is no honour.

Benjamin Disraeli

President Bush was renowned for his difficulties with the English language . . .

You cannot be President of the United States if you don't have faith. Remember Lincoln, going to his knees in times of trial and the civil war and all that stuff. You can't be. And we are blessed. So don't feel sorry for – don't cry for me Argentina.

Stressing the importance of praying to New Hampshire voters

It has been said by some cynic, maybe it was a former President, 'If you want a friend in Washington get a dog.' We took them literally – that advice – as you know. But I didn't need that because I have Barbara.

I've got to run now and relax. The doctor told me to relax. The doctor told me to relax. The doctor told me. He was the one. He said 'relax'.

At the end of a press conference

When I need a little free advice about Saddam Hussein I turn to country music.

At an awards ceremony in Nashville

I don't want to get, you know, here we are close to the election – sounding a knell of overconfidence that I don't feel.

In an interview with Sir David Frost

Boy they were big crematoriums weren't they?

During a visit to Auschwitz

I've got to be careful I don't overcheerlead on this economy.

There's no difference between me and the President [Reagan] on taxes. No more nit-picking. Zip-ah-dee-doo-dah. Now it's off to the races!

The Democrats want to ram it down my ear in a political victory.

I put confidence in the American people, in their ability to sort through what is fair and what is unfair, what is ugly and unugly.

Top Ten Quotes from President Reagan

Please tell me you're Republicans.

To surgeons as he entered the operating room, 30 March 1981

History teaches that wars begin when governments believe the price of aggression is cheap.

16 January 1984

We will always remember. We will always be proud. We will always be prepared, so we may always be free.

Normandy, 6 June 1984

We will never forget them, nor the last time we saw them – this morning, as they prepared for their journey, and waved goodbye and slipped the surly bonds of earth to touch the face of God.

Speech about the Challenger disaster, 28 January 28 1986

Government's view of the economy could be summed up in a few short phrases: If it moves, tax it. If it keeps moving, regulate it. And if it stops moving, subsidise it.

15 August 1986

The other day, someone told me the difference between a democracy and a people's democracy. It's the same difference as between a jacket and a strait-jacket.

10 December 1986

A friend of mine was asked to a costume ball a short time ago. He slapped some egg on his face and went as a liberal economist.

11 February 1987

How do you tell a Communist? Well, it's someone who reads Marx and Lenin. And how do you tell an anti-Communist? It's someone who understands Marx and Lenin.

25 September 1987

Mr Gorbachev, open this gate. Mr Gorbachev, tear down this wall.

Berlin, 12 June 1987

Welfare's purpose should be to eliminate, as far as possible, the need for its own existence.

7 January 1970

Top Ten Politicians' Comments on the Spice Girls

I think I've heard of them very vaguely ... They're not lesbians are they?
George Walden

Of course I know the Spice Girls. There's posters all over London. But I'm not led to make serious speculation about Spice Girl meanings.
Peter Lilley MP

Perhaps the Spice Girls are the last vestige of eighties self-interest and self-gratification.
Michael Connarty MP

I have teenage children and I know one Spice Girls song which is rather good. It goes 'If you want to get my something or other, then you better get it together baby' ... I sing all these pop songs about the house and then my daughter will tell me that the words have got all these dreadful hidden meanings.
Gary Streeter

I saw them briefly the other day on Des O'Connor. They were a bit giggly and I turned it over. My taste is Meat Loaf.
Kevin Barron MP

Oh, they're straight from the shoulder and refreshing. I would call them the Spicer Girls. Bare midriffs. I'd love to have these girls canvassing with me. Do I get my wrists slapped if I call them girls? Of course, Margaret Thatcher was the first.
James Spicer

Like Margaret Thatcher they are here-today-gone-tomorrow entertainers.
Simon Hughes MP

Whether they're a reflection of their contemporaries is hard to see. They sound pretty vacuous women to me.
Kim Howells MP

I'm not up to date on the pop chart. I'm just a bit concerned they're not the group I condemned for doing all sorts of nasty lesbian things on stage.
Female Tory MP

I've been a secret Spice Girls' fan for a long time.
Michael Portillo

Top Ten Quotes on Political Leadership

You do not lead by hitting people over the head – that's assault, not leadership.

Dwight Eisenhower

The boss says 'go'. The leader says 'let's go'.

Dwight Eisenhower

Leadership means not having to be completely in harmony with everyone else.

Winston Churchill

I start with the premise that the function of leadership is to produce more leaders, not more followers.

Ralph Nader, US political activist

I must follow them. I am their leader.

Andrew Bonar Law, Prime Minister, 1921

A leader takes people where they want to go. A great leader takes people where they don't necessarily want to go, but where they ought to be.

Rosalynn Carter, US First Lady, 1977–81

A leader must be able to concentrate under difficult conditions, to keep his head when all around him are losing theirs.

Ross Perot

A leader is a dealer in hope.

Napoleon Bonaparte

Use power to help people. For we are given power not to advance our own purposes not to make a great show in the world, nor a name. There is but one just use of power and it is to serve the people.

George Bush

The art of leadership is saying no, not yes. It is very easy to say yes.

Tony Blair

Top Ten Memorable One-liners from Norman Tebbit

Third Best. It's called 'going for bronze' I believe.

On the Alliance's Going for Gold slogan in the 1987 election

He likes to pose as Margaret Thatcher in drag to pick up Tory votes.

On David Owen

Those who stand outside the town hall and scream and throw rotten eggs are not the real unemployed. If they were really hard up they would be eating them.

Why don't you go and have another heart attack?

To Labour MP Tom Litterick

I use the word 'neuter' when I talk about what I am doing to the trade unions because I've been told I mustn't use the vernacular.

Take a sedative.

To Denis Healey

As usual you have spent more time with your mouth open rather than your ears.

To Dennis Skinner

I'm older than you are sonny and you can take me on when you grow up.

To Neil Kinnock

I grew up in the thirties with our unemployed father. He did not riot. He got on his bike and looked for work.

Speech at Tory Party Conference, 15 October 1981

The cricket test – which side do they cheer for? Are you still looking back to where you came from or where you are?

On the loyalties of British immigrants

Top Ten Tony Banks Quotes

He is to the arts what 'Bonecrusher' Smith is to lepidoptery. His views are philistine in the extreme, anachronistic and wholly unacceptable to any civilised body of thought.

On Tory MP Terry Dicks

Woolly-hatted, muesli-eating, Tory lick-spittles.

On Liberal Democrats

It will pay for next year's gin supply.

On the increase in the Queen Mother's civil list allowance. Sunday Times, *18 May 1997*

My epitaph will be: He Was a Complete Tosser.

I most certainly do not bother to read my speeches because I know what a load of rubbish they are before anybody hears them.

To make things worse, they [The Tories] have elected a foetus as leader. I bet a lot of them wish they had not voted against abortion now.

September 30 1997

It's not fair to kick a man when he's down, but it's safer isn't it?

On Peter Mandelson's failure to be elected to the NEC

Arrogant, self-satisfied, smug and complacent individual [who composes] pretty forgettable chocolate box stuff.

On Andrew Lloyd Webber, Daily Telegraph, *19 September 1997*

It's very foolish to criticise Paddy (Ashdown) because he can kill with his bare hands.

Daily Telegraph, *10 May 1997*

If I could afford it I would only drink champagne.

Quoted in Sunday Times *18 May 1997*

Top Ten Conservative–Conservative Insults

Mr Chamberlain who looked and spoke like a cheese-monger.

Benjamin Disraeli on Joseph Chamberlain

She has done as much for our party as King Herod did for baby sitting.

Andrew Mackay on Edwina Currie

Margaret Thatcher and Ted Heath both have a great vision. The difference is that Margaret Thatcher has a vision that Britain will one day be great again, and Ted Heath has a vision that one day Ted Heath will be great again.

Robert Jones

He is forever poised between a cliché and an indiscretion.

Harold Macmillan on Sir Anthony Eden

Receiving support from Ted Heath in a by-election is like being measured by an undertaker.

George Gardiner

Reminds me of the expression my mother used: 'Empty vessels make the most noise.'

Anne Winterton on Edwina Currie

The immaculate misconception.

Norman St John Stevas on Margaret Thatcher

He has the lucidity which is the by-product of a fundamentally sterile mind.

Aneurin Bevan on Neville Chamberlain

I wouldn't say she was open-minded on the Middle East, so much as empty-headed. She probably thinks Sinai is the plural of sinus.

Jonathan Aitken on Margaret Thatcher

Decided only to be undecided, resolved to be irresolute, adamant for drift, solid for fluidity, all-powerful to be impotent.

Winston Churchill on Stanley Baldwin

Top Ten Labour–Conservative Insults

A bounder, a liar, a deceiver, a cheat, a crook.

Tam Dalyell on Margaret Thatcher after the sinking of the Belgrano

A semi-housetrained polecat.

Michael Foot on Norman Tebbit

Like a boil on a verruca.

Neil Kinnock on Norman Tebbit

The Prime Minister tells us she has given the French President a piece of her mind – not a gift I would receive with alacrity.

Denis Healey on Margaret Thatcher

They are nothing else but a load of kippers – two-faced with no guts.

Eric Heffer

Meeting David Mellor is like being hit in the face with a mouthful of Brylcreem.

John Edmonds on David Mellor

Putting Norman Tebbit in charge of industrial relations is like appointing Dracula to take charge of blood transfusions.

Eric Varley on Norman Tebbit

Fifty per cent genius – fifty per cent bloody fool.

Clement Attlee on Winston Churchill

Lower than vermin.

Aneurin Bevan on Conservatives

He is undoubtedly living proof that a pig's bladder on a stick can be elected as a Member of Parliament.

Tony Banks on Terry Dicks

Top Ten Conservative–Labour Insults

The self-appointed king of the gutter.

Michael Heseltine on Neil Kinnock

He is a sheep in sheep's clothing.

Winston Churchill on Clement Attlee

As far as the fourteenth Earl is concerned, I suppose that Mr Wilson, when you come to think of it, is the fourteenth Mr Wilson.

Sir Alec Douglas-Home in 1963

The Honourable Member for two tube stations.

Sir Nicholas Fairbairn on Frank Dobson (MP for Holborn and St Pancras)

A tardy little marionette.

Randolph Churchill on Clement Attlee

The voters are not daft. They can smell a rat whether it is wrapped up in a red flag or covered in roses.

Norman Tebbit

The inherent virtue of Socialism is the equal sharing of miseries.

Winston Churchill

Far better to keep your mouth shut and let every one think you're stupid than to open it and leave no doubt.

Norman Tebbit on Dennis Skinner

The boneless wonder.

Winston Churchill on Ramsay MacDonald

Neil Kinnock's speeches go on for so long because he has nothing to say, so he has no way of knowing when he has finished saying it.

John Major on Neil Kinnock

Top Ten Labour–Labour Insults

A guide to Bennite Britain – not so much a labour of love as a premature ejaculation.

Austen Mitchell on Labour's 1983 election manifesto

He's just a little man who's been stupid.

George Brown on Harold Wilson after his 1976 resignation

He just cannot be allowed to go on rushing round like a demented Santa Claus, scattering imaginary tenners from his sleigh.

Neil Kinnock on Michael Meacher

A kind of ageing, perennial tough who immatures with age.

Harold Wilson on Tony Benn

As Moses he would have mistimed his arrival at the parting of the waters.

Austin Mitchell on Jim Callaghan

He seems determined to make a trumpet sound like a tin whistle. He brings to the fierce struggle of politics the tepid enthusiasm of a lazy summer afternoon at a cricket match.

Aneurin Bevan on Clement Attlee

He is quite stoically bland. The sheer blandness is so totally inherent that it is quite difficult to embarrass him.

Brian Sedgemore on Tony Blair

Nye's little dog.

Hugh Dalton on Harold Wilson

A desiccating calculating machine.

Aneurin Bevan on Hugh Gaitskell

Sit down man, you're a bloody tragedy.

James Maxton to Ramsay MacDonald

Top Ten Things Politicians Said and Wished They Hadn't

No woman in my time will be Prime Minister or Foreign Secretary – not the top jobs. Anyway I wouldn't want to be Prime Minister. You have to give yourself one hundred per cent to the job.

Margaret Thatcher

Solidarity is undermining the Socialist State of Poland.

Arthur Scargill

One feels that Uganda cannot afford General Amin's warm-hearted generosity.

The Times

I have the thermometer in my mouth and I am listening to it all the time.

William Whitelaw

Most of the egg production in this country sadly is now infected with salmonella.

Edwina Currie, 1988

There is no Soviet domination of Eastern Europe, and there never will be under a Ford administration.

President Ford, 1976

We'll negotiate a withdrawal from the EEC which has drained our natural resources and destroyed jobs.

Tony Blair, 1983

Je ne regrette rien.

Norman Lamont

Go back to your constituencies and prepare for government.

David Steel

Read my lips, no new taxes.

President Bush, 1988

Part Seven

Sex, Money
and
Scandal

WITH A NOD TO
MAGRITTE

Ten Politicians Women Find Most Attractive

1. Peter Mandelson
2. Paddy Ashdown
3. Tony Blair
4. Michael Portillo
5. Stephen Dorrell
6. Gordon Brown
7. John Redwood
8. Michael Heseltine
9. John Major
10. Ken Livingstone

Source: NOP, November 1996

Ten Politicians Women Find Most Unattractive

1. David Mellor
2. John Prescott
3. John Major
4. Ken Livingstone
5. Michael Heseltine
6. Dennis Skinner
7. David Blunkett
8. Kenneth Clarke
9. Michael Howard
10. Jack Straw

Source: NOP, November 1996

Ten Politicians *Forum* Magazine Readers Find Sexy

Tony Blair (25% males, 35% females)
Virginia Bottomley (35% males, 15% females)
Harriet Harman (30% males, 20% females)
Michael Portillo (30% males, 20% females)
Clare Short (15% males, 15% females)
Paddy Ashdown (8% males, 13% females)
Diane Abbott (10% males, 10% females)
Betty Boothroyd (10% males, 10% females)
John Major (5% males, 15 % females)
Gordon Brown (10% males, 10% females)

Source: *Forum* Magazine, 1994

Eight Politicians *Forum* Magazine Readers Find a Turn-off

Margaret Beckett (45% males, 50% females)
Robin Cook (35% males, 30% females)
Ken Clarke (15% males, 40% females)
Virginia Bottomley (25% males, 25% females)
John Major (30% males, 15% females)
Clare Short (20% males, 25% females)
Norman Fowler (15% males, 5% females)
Douglas Hurd (5% males, 10% females)

Source: *Forum* Magazine 1994

Thirteen Politicians Involved in Gay Scandals

Lord Harcourt	Liberal Peer who committed suicide in 1922
Earl Beauchamp	Fled abroad in 1931
Lord Farquhar	Involved in homosexual scandal
William Field	Caught in public lavatories
Ian Harvey	Accused of importuning a guardsman in St James' Park
Jeremy Thorpe	Accused of gay affair with male model Norman Scott
Keith Hampson	Found not guilty of indecently assaulting police-man
Allan Roberts	Accused of sex offences with teenage youths
Harvey Proctor	Fined £1,450 for spanking rent boys
Alan Amos	Arrested for but not charged with indecency
Michael Brown	Only came out after tabloids exposed affair with youth
Jerry Hayes	Research Assistant sold story of alleged gay affair
Michael Hirst	Resigned as Tory Party Chairman in Scotland

Ten Signs You're in Love with a Politician

1. When you see him on TV you start licking the screen
2. You call the Parliamentary Channel requesting a tape of his greatest speeches
3. You fantasize about Black Rod
4. You write to the Queen suggesting his birthday is declared a national holiday
5. You just luuuurve those double chins
6. You're turned on by the sight of his despatch box
7. You buy up remaindered copies of his memoirs so his feelings won't be hurt
8. You tell all your friends that his wife just doesn't understand him
9. You spend all your holidays in his constituency
10. You'd give him your last Rolo

Ten David Mellor Campaign Slogans

1. I promise I'll keep my pants on
2. No worse than Paddy Ashdown
3. Four fewer than Steven Norris
4. Because everyone deserves another chance
5. Come up and see my CD collection
6. All aboard the 606
7. He won't take the Chelsea shirt off your back
8. I'm only in it for the babes
9. David Mellor – any time, any place, anywhere
10. Paaaarty!

Ten Politicians' Chat-up Lines

1. Would you like to see the contents of my despatch box?
2. Have you ever had a whip?
3. Hello, I'm David Mellor
4. I've asked Angie to join us, you don't mind do you?
5. I've asked Bobby to join us, you don't mind do you?
6. I'm so depressed about the world crisis I really don't think I should spend tonight alone
7. In your honour I'm naming 1997 the International Year of the Babe
8. Hi there. My name's, er, Martin
9. Ever done it in the lobby?
10. You know what they say about Black Rod?

Ten Conservative Political Turn-ons

1. Matron
2. St Trinian's films
3. Mrs Thatcher
4. Edwina Currie's legs
5. Dame Janet Fookes
6. Joanna Lumley
7. Euroboys
8. William Hague's bald patch
9. Alan Duncan's winsome smile
10. Cecil Parkinson's leer

Ten Old Labour Political Turn-ons

1. Tony Benn
2. Mushy peas
3. Whippets
4. Flat caps
5. Miners
6. Sheffield
7. Dennis Skinner's eyes
8. Glorious election defeats
9. Alma Sedgwick
10. Marx's *Das Kapital*

Ten New Labour Political Turn-ons

1. Tony Blair
2. Avocado dip
3. The chairs at Pont de la Tour
4. The grass on Hampstead Heath
5. John Prescott's love handles
6. Harriet Harman's hemline
7. Stephen Twigg's mane
8. Peter Mandelson's bottom
9. Tessa Jowell's pout
10. Dawn Primarolo's school mistress act

Top Twenty Visually Challenged Politicians (and we don't mean they need glasses)

1. David Mellor
2. John Bowis
3. Douglas Hogg
4. Robin Cook
5. Ann Widdecombe
6. Donald Anderson
7. Patrick Cormack
8. Norman Baker
9. Jackie Ballard
10. Margaret Beckett
11. Andrew Bennett
12. Clive Betts
13. Malcolm Chisholm
14. Charles Clarke
15. Gwynneth Dunwoody
16. George Howarth
17. Ian McCartney
18. Peter Pike
19. Brian Iddon
20. John Gummer

Top Twenty Most Good-looking Male Politicians

1. Michael Portillo
2. Cecil Parkinson
3. Stephen Twigg
4. Steve Norris
5. John Bercow
6. Tony Blair
7. Michael Moore
8. Nicholas St Aubyn
9. Ben Bradshaw
10. Alistair Darling
11. David Davis
12. Alan Duncan
13. Liam Fox
14. Andrew George
15. Bernard Jenkin
16. Christopher Leslie
17. Andrew MacKay
18. Michael Meacher
19. Michael Foster
20. Shaun Woodward

Top Twenty Most Good-looking Female Politicians

1. Oona King
2. Virginia Bottomley
3. Siobhain McDonagh
4. Anne McIntosh
5. Julie Kirkbride
6. Tessa Jowell
7. Harriet Harman
8. Caroline Flint
9. Dawn Primarolo
10. Charlotte Atkins
11. Judith Church
12. Yvette Cooper
13. Elizabeth Blackman
14. Jean Corston
15. Angela Browning
16. Joan Ruddock
17. Claire Ward
18. Angela Eagle
19. Maria Eagle
20. Karen Buck

Top Ten Politicians Gays Find Attractive

1. Michael Portillo
2. Peter Lilley
3. Margaret Thatcher
4. John Redwood
5. Stephen Twigg
6. Ben Bradshaw
7. Matthew Taylor
8. Sebastian Coe
9. Claire Short
10. Peter Mandelson

Part Eight

More UNOFFICIAL

Lists

Ten Fictional Works Featuring Margaret Thatcher

1. *God and All His Angels* (novel by Graham Lord)
2. *Titmuss Regained* (novel by John Mortimer)
3. *First Among Equals* (novel by Jeffrey Archer)
4. *New Statesman* (Yorkshire TV)
5. *The Negotiator* (novel by Frederick Forsyth)
6. *Operation 10* (novel by Hardiman Scott)
7. *Anyone for Denis* (West End comedy)
8. *XPD* (novel by Len Deighton)
9. *Electric Beach* (novel by Laurence Rees)
10. *The Child in Time* (novel by Ian McEwan)

MPs' Eight Most Over-rated Authors

1. Jeffrey Archer
2. Salman Rushdie
3. Henry James
4. Martin Amis
5. D H Lawrence
6. Karl Marx
7. Enid Blyton
8. Iris Murdoch

Source: Dillons survey, 1996

MPs' Four Greatest Political Books Ever

1. *The Prince* – Machiavelli
2. The *Ragged Trousered Philanthropists* – Robert Tressell
3. *On Liberty* – J S Mill
4. *Diaries* – Alan Clark

Source: Dillons survey, 1996

MPs' Favourite Ever Books

1. The Bible
2. *Pride and Prejudice* – Jane Austen
3. *The Lord of the Rings* – Tolkein
4. *The Iliad* – Homer
5. *Germinal* – Emile Zola
6. *Modern Times* – Paul Johnson

Source: Dillons survey, 1996

MPs' Favourite Ever Authors

1. Alexander Solzhenitsyn
2. Martin Amis
3. Doris Lessing
4. Colin Thubron
5. Gore Vidal
6. David Lodge

Source: Dillons survey, 1996

Ten Author Politicians

1. **Rupert Allason** – Author of various worthy tomes on spies and counter-intelligence under the pen name Nigel West. Elected for Torbay in 1992 but lost by only twelve votes in 1997.

2. **Jeffrey Archer** – The author 'daddy' of them all. Jeffrey Archer was MP for Louth from 1969–74 1980s was appointed Deputy Chairman of the Conservative Party in 1986. Has written a dozen novels, many containing a political plot.

3. **Gyles Brandreth** – More famous for his jumpers on the late, lamented TVam, the former MP for Chester has penned a couple of novels as well as a rather early autobiography. None of them troubled the Top Ten Bestsellers lists.

4. **Vaclav Havel** – President of the Czech Republic and all-round good egg, Mr Havel's superb plays have now almost been forgotten as his political career has eclipsed his writing.

5. **Douglas Hurd** – Co-authored several excellent works of fiction in the early 1970s with Andrew Osmond. Rumoured to be working on a new one at the moment.

6. **Edwina Currie** – 'Bonkbusteress extraordinaire' her tails of kinky sex in the Commons were secretly read, by most MPs but only a few would ever admit to it.

7. **Tim Renton** – Former Tory Chief Whip is the author of two books with a political plot. Now in competition with his wife, who has also penned a political novel.

8. **Benjamin Disraeli** – Even more famous than Jeffrey Archer in his day. If Disraeli ever wanted to read a book, he wrote one.

9. **Michael Dobbs** – Formerly Norman Tebbit's chief of staff at Conservative Central Office, Dobbs shot to fame for his trilogy featuring the outwardly urbane yet cunningly clever Chief Whip Francis Urquhart.

10. **Newt Gingrich** – US Speaker of the House of Representatives who also wrote a novel called *1945*. Truly awful.

Top Ten Ways of Spotting a Bleeding Heart Liberal

1. You go pink with rage at the thought of paedophiles being executed, but defend the killing of unborn children as an expression of choice
2. You believe animals can think, trees have feelings and the foetus is a blob of protoplasm
3. You don't believe in marriage, except for homosexuals
4. You are quite happy to legalise drugs and outlaw handguns
5. You are permanently 'worried' about things and you use the word 'community' a lot
6. You don't think Gerry Adams is all bad
7. You think the rehabilitation of criminals is more important than punishing them
8. You think that whatever their level, taxes should be increased
9. Gordon Brown's neo-indigenous growth theory turns you on
10. You don't understand people who are against positive discrimination and are more than happy to sacrifice someone else's job to assuage your own guilt

Ten Things You Always Wanted to Know About *The Economist*

1. Economists rarely read it
2. It's got two lovely staples
3. It looks good on your coffee table
4. Comes with a very elegant binder
5. Easy to throw away
6. Has a number at the top of each page
7. Its predictions are rarely worth taking much notice of
8. Has a nice picture and witty slogan on the cover
9. Tries desperately to compete with *Time* but can't
10. It's not American, though you could be forgiven for wondering

Craig Brown's Top Ten Least Likely Political Headlines

1. 'But That's Enough About Me' – Exclusive interview with Jeffrey Archer
2. Two Sides to Every Question Argues Paisley
3. Jack Straw Makes Interesting Point
4. Thatcher's Shock Admission: I Am No Longer Prime Minister
5. I May Be Some Time – Antarctic Survivors Find Edwina Currie Note
6. Saddam Admits Moustache 'Big Mistake' – Agrees to Shave
7. Tory MP in Two-in-a-Bed Love Romp With Own Wife
8. More Money Than Sense – St John of Fawsley Slams Royal Family
9. Sir Edward Heath Wakes Early to Bag Poolside Lounger Before Germans
10. Lord Owen Goes It Alone Then Splits With Self

Top Ten Ways Politicians Avoid Answering the Question

1. Ignoring the question
2. Acknowledging the question without answering
3. Questioning the question
4. Attacking the question

5. Attacking the interviewer
6. Declining to answer
7. Giving an incomplete answer
8. Repeating the previous answer
9. Claiming to have already answered the question
10. Making a political point

Ten Ways Margaret Thatcher Stalled Interviewers

1. No, please let me go on
2. May I just finish
3. One moment
4. I must beg of you
5. Will you give me time
6. May I now and then say a word in my own defence
7. I would love to go on
8. Please, there's just another thing
9. No, don't stop me
10. No, let me stand up for my government

Source, Dr Peter Bull and Kate Meyer: 'How Margaret Thatcher and Neil Kinnock Avoid Answering Questions in Political Interviews', 1988.

Margaret Thatcher's Desert Island Discs

Emperor Piano Concerto by Beethoven
Dvořak's 'Going Home' from *New World Symphony*
Excerpts from Verdi's *Aida*
'Nutty Walt', a Bob Newhardt comedy sketch
'Smoke Gets In Your Eyes' by Irene Dunn
Elijah by Felix Mendelssohn
Andante for Trumpet by Saint Preux
'Easter Hymn' from *Cavalleria Rusticana* by Mascagni

Neil Kinnock's Desert Island Discs

Byrn Calfaria
'Di quella Pira' from Verdi's opera *Il Trovatore*
'Serenade' from Bizet's opera *The Fair Maid of Perth*
Symphony Number 1 by Brahms
'Wake Up Little Susie' by Simon and Garfunkel
'Imagine' by John Lennon
'Yada Yada' by Dory Previn
'Horace the Horse' sung by his two-year-old daughter Rachel

Tony Blair's Desert Island Discs

'Cancel Today' by Ezio
'Wishing Well' by Free
'Fourth of July, Ashbury Park' by Bruce Springsteen
Love theme from *Elephant Man*
Adagio for Strings by Samuel Barber
Clair de Lune by Debussy
'In my Life' by the Beatles
'Cross Road Blues' by Robert Johnson

Ten Questions Not to Ask . . .

John Major: How many O Levels have you got?
Paddy Ashdown: How come we can't see your eyes?
Tony Blair: Where do you get your teeth polished?
Cherie Booth: How much has playing the dutiful wife cost you in lost fees?
John Prescott: I suppose a gin and tonic is out of the question?
Margaret Thatcher: Did John Major really have a problem with his wisdom teeth?
Jack Cunningham: What do you do all day?
Cecil Parkinson: So, do you think the Child Support Agency has been a success?

Gordon Brown: So what's the story with your chin?
Nicholas Soames: So what's the story with your chins?

Joe Joseph's Top Ten Political Medical Complaints

Alexia: Word blindness, or Tony Blair's inability to pronounce certain words – specifically 'Socialism'.

Compulsive talking: Starts with grimaces and progresses to involuntary comments as the affliction worsens, often culminating in episodes of coprolalia (using foul language) while watching *Election Call* on TV especially when Gordon Brown or Michael Howard are in the hot seat.

Glossectomy: Removal of all or part of the tongue, often prescribed by Peter Mandelson for John Prescott, Diane Abbott and Ken Livingstone.

Halitosis: Insulting odour emitted when a manifesto promise emerging from a politician's mouth is so implausible that it stinks.

Infantile spasms: Seizure induced in politicians by Jeremy Paxman repeatedly barking the phrase, 'For God's sake, answer the bloody question!'

Irritable colon: Pain in the backside, such as Jack Straw in his sanctimonious moods.

Premature ejaculation: Unguarded comment made by a Labour politician that is later 'explained more fully' by Labour's rapid rebuttal unit.

Premeditation: Disease that erupts around the dinner table when everyone suddenly becomes convinced they know the outcome of the election.

Sadomasochism: The condition in which you switch over to ITN's *News at Ten* even though you have watched the BBC1's specially extended *Nine O'Clock News*. If you then switch to BBC 2's *Newsnight* you should consult a specialist.

Scotoma: An area of abnormal vision, suffered by Paddy Ashdown and a few other Liberal Democrat candidates who believe they might form the next government.

With kind permission of Joe Joseph and Times Newspapers Limited, first published 25 April 1997.

Eighteen Biographies of Margaret Thatcher

1975   *Margaret Thatcher: First Lady of the House*, Ernle Money, Leslie Frewin

1975   *Margaret Thatcher*, George Gardiner MP, William Kimber

1975   *Margaret Thatcher: A Personal and Political Biography*, Russell Lewis, Routledge

1978   *Margaret Thatcher: A Tory and Her Party*, Patrick Cosgrave, Hutchinson

1978   *Margaret Thatcher: A Profile*, Patricia Murray, W H Allen

1979   *Madam Prime Minister*, Allan Mayer, Newsweek Books (US)

1983   *Thatcher*, Nicholas Wapshott and George Brock, Macdonald

1983   *Margaret Thatcher: Wife, Mother, Politician*, Penny Junor, Sidgwick and Jackson

1984   *Margaret Thatcher: A Study in Power*, Bruce Arnold, Hamish Hamilton

1985   *Thatcher: The First Term*, Patrick Cosgrave, Bodley Head

1988   *Thatcher*, Kenneth Harris, Weidenfeld and Nicolson

1989   *Margaret Thatcher: The Woman Within*, Andrew Thomson, W H Allen

1989   *Margaret Daughter of Beatrice*, Leo Abse, Jonathan Cape

1989   *One of Us*, Hugo Young, Macmillan

1990   *Maggie: An Intimate Portrait of a Woman in Power*, Chris Ogden, Simon and Schuster (US)

1992   *Margaret Thatcher in Victory and Downfall*, Bruce Geelhoed, Praeger (US)

1993   *The Downing Street Years*, Margaret Thatcher, HarperCollins

1995   *The Path to Power*, Margaret Thatcher, HarperCollins

Ten Things John Major Won't Say Sorry For

1. Sacking Norman Lamont
2. Goosing Gillian Shephard after the last Cabinet meeting
3. That clumsy overture he made to Sue Lawley
4. Tucking his shirt into his underpants
5. Spreading rumours about Tony Blair's imminent baldness
6. Recording a song called 'Nobody Loves a Loser'

7. Having three-in-a-bed fantasies about Ian Botham and a cricket bat
8. Leaving those chewing gum relics under the Number Ten sitting-room carpet
9. Liking peas
10. Terry Major-Ball

Politicians Who Have Appeared in the Movies or on TV Playing Themselves

Ed Koch (*The Muppets Take Manhattan*, 1984)
Michael Foot (*Rockets Galore*, 1958)
Gough Whitlam (*Barry McKenzie Holds His Own*, 1974)
Hubert Humphrey (*The Candidate*, 1972)
Yitzhak Rabin (*Operation Thunderbolt*, 1977)
Harold Macmillan (*The Archers*)
Margaret Thatcher (*Yes, Prime Minister* sketch, 1984)
Nancy Astor (*Royal Cavalcade*, 1935)
Bella Abzug (*Manhattan*, 1979)
Sebastian Coe (*The Brittas Empire*, 1993)
George McGovern (*The Candidate*, 1972)
Hubert Humphrey (*The Candidate*, 1972)

Nine Actors Who Have Played Margaret Thatcher

Sylvia Sims   Steve Nallon
Janet Hargreaves   Mike Yarwood
Janet Brown   June Whitfield
Faith Brown   Maureen Lipman
Angela Thorne

Ten Campaign Promises Tony Blair Is Sorry He Made

1. To bomb France back to the First Republic
2. To privatise the British Library through QVC
3. To bring more lightweight pretty boys into the Party
4. To reveal at first Prime Minister's questions John Prescott's IQ
5. To abandon the use of verbs
6. To invite Tony Booth to the victory celebrations
7. To give an interview to Dr Ruth
8. Not to raise taxes
9. A referendum on PR – Paddy can go to hell
10. To make Frank Dobson Secretary of State for Health

Ten John Major Excuses for Losing the Election

1. Blamed Norma for that hideous lipstick
2. He just knew May Day wasn't such a good day to hold an election
3. Brian Mawhinney didn't smile enough at press conferences
4. Number plate on election battle bus read DUD 1
5. Michael Brunson kept using the words Major and 'loser' in the same sentence on *News at Ten*
6. Forgot to wear lucky underpants
7. Used Geoffrey Howe to warm up campaign crowds
8. Three-day campaign tour on Guernsey was a mistake
9. Fell for Blair's 'You vote for me and I'll vote for you' pledge
10. An endorsement from former Canadian PM Kim Campbell was maybe not such a good idea

Ten Ways for William Hague to Make Himself More Exciting

1. Kill a man with kung fu kick on *Panorama*
2. Dump Ffion and marry her fourteen-year-old cousin
3. Change campaign slogan from 'Fresh Start' to 'Fresh Beaver'
4. Answer questions on *Question Time* with 'D'know, I was too pissed to remember'

5. Hang out with Liam Gallacher
6. Shave head completely – might as well anyway
7. Outdo Blair by refusing to use nouns as well as verbs
8. Take weekend break on Club 18-30 holiday in Benidorm
9. Go to celeb party with Tiffany from *EastEnders*
10. Go on *Stars in Their Eyes* and say, 'And tonight Matthew, I'm going to be Shirley Bassey'

Ten Ways to Make Communism Fun Again

1. Spell it with a K
2. Have Castro do a guest slot on the *Clive Anderson Show*
3. Add mechanical shark attraction at Lenin's Tomb
4. Have Christian Dior introduce new 'Khmer Rouge'
5. Give everybody red birthmark to wear on forehead
6. Have Deng Xiaoping cry during interview with Selina Scott
7. Less centralised economic planning, more PARTY!
8. Free vodka
9. Rename St Petersburg 'Leningrad in association with McDonald's'
10. Free Brezhnev eyebrow makeovers

Ten Reasons to Increase MPs' Salaries

1. Many big companies are cutting back on bribes
2. Most Soho bars have raised their cover charges
3. Our nation's lawmakers ought to make at least one tenth of Kermit the Frog's income
4. To keep the money out of the hands of those undeserving nurses and teachers
5. Even an estate agent earns more
6. Mistresses are expensive
7. That new Daimler just eats up the petrol
8. Leather costs
9. Consultancy just isn't what it used to be
10. That bastard Nolan

Ten Reasons to Vote

1. The chance to take a deep breath in a high school gymnasium
2. Good practice for voting for *A Song for Europe*
3. So you'll feel personally involved when your MP is hauled off to jail
4. Even though it's never come close to happening, your one vote could make a difference
5. You'll feel so self-righteous if the other lot get in and muck things up
6. If you don't vote you can't whinge about how terrible things are
7. You get a kick out of spoiling your ballot paper
8. You hate to be in the minority
9. You just love giving a false polling number to the saddos outside the polling station
10. If you can't beat 'em . . .

Ten Ways France Is Preparing for a Single Currency

1. Dialing 999
2. Kissing plenty of German ass
3. Going a really long time without a shower
4. Installing speed bumps to slow the Panzers down
5. Cutting bedsheets into easy to wave white rectangles
6. Shaving armpits in celebration
7. Preparing TV Documentary on why the Brits needn't have bothered on June 6 1944
8. Nicole tells Papa to trade in the Clio for a Merc
9. President Chirac proposes changing the country's name to West Germany
10. Charles de Gaulle turns in his grave

Ten Signs That You're Politically Correct

1. You're a white male, but feel very guilty about it
2. You separate all your rubbish into different containers for recycling

3. You make sure that your make-up has not been tested on animals
4. Your CD collection includes mandatory discs by KD Lang, U2, REM, Sinead O'Connor and Sting
5. You believe that if an animal is cute, furry, huggable or rare then it has rights
6. You used phrases like, 'Isn't that pot called the Kettle Afro-Caribbean?'
7. You can't abide *Men Behaving Badly*
8. You don't go ape when you find out your daughter has tried marijuana even though you want to
9. You watch BBC2 documentaries on the third world even though in your heart of hearts you know you'll be dead bored
10. You don't really mind if your local council gives money to one-legged black disabled lesbian groups

Ten Things Which Would Be Different if the Prime Minister Were a Dog

1. Labour Party HQ replaced by twenty-storey-high fire hydrant
2. Abolition of *Pets Mean Prizes*
3. Capital punishment restored for Dale Winton
4. Doggy door on Number Ten
5. Dog biscuits on the NHS
6. Compulsory sterilisation for all cats
7. Life sentences for tail dockers
8. Battersea Dogs' Home to be renovated and replace Chequers as PM's country residence
9. First Lady to be renamed First Bitch
10. PM to have the mandatory right to shag the legs of all fellow Cabinet Ministers

Ten Ways Cherie Blair Could Improve Her Image

1. Move her eyes closer together
2. Never be seen with Hillary Clinton
3. Appear on TV as Julia Brogan in *Brookside*
4. Have an operation to remove the 666 from her scalp
5. Make prank call to Tony on the *Jimmy Young Show* pretending to be a secret lover
6. Stop wearing the 'All men are stupid' T-shirt
7. Comb her hair
8. Get rid of THAT nightie
9. When kissing Tony in public, get the timing right
10. Learn to buy her kids some decent clothes

Ten Football Personalities Who Vote Conservative

1. Ken Bates
2. Sir John Hall
3. Jimmy Greaves
4. John Barnes
5. Gerry Francis
6. Tony Cottee
7. Emlyn Hughes
8. Lawrie McMenemy
9. Terry Venables
10. Er, David Mellor

Ten Things in Politics You Would Have Thought Impossible Ten Years Ago

1. Margaret Thatcher isn't Prime Minister any more
2. John Major was
3. The coal mines would be privatised
4. What the European Commission says, goes
5. John Prescott would be taken seriously
6. Neil Kinnock would be a European Commissioner
7. A goblin is Foreign Secretary
8. Teresa Gorman would still be fifty-three
9. South Africa would be ruled by Nelson Mandela
10. The Russians are now our allies

Ten Signs Your MP Is Going Mad

1. He appears concerned about his constituents
2. Demonstrates his support for the beef industry by force-feeding beefburgers to his seven-year-old daughter
3. Complains that Disraeli won't reply to his letters
4. He wants to be called Glenda
5. Demands that each of the seventy-four voices in his head deserves a vote
6. You live in Billericay
7. Introduces a Bill to replace the National Anthem with 'On the Good Ship Lollypop'
8. Urges the despatch of a brigade of Boy Scouts to retake France
9. He seriously thought John Redwood would help him win
10. He supports the introduction of a windfall tax

Ten Favourite Westminster Haunts for Politicians

1. **L'Amico** – Italian restaurant on Horseferry Road, popular for conspiratorial lunches.
2. **Greens** – Upmarket, slightly stuffy restaurant in Marsham Street popular with Tories and lobbyists.
3. **Atrium** – Airy restaurant at 4 Millbank. Frequented by lobbyists, journalists and MPs in equal numbers. Food great, service awfully slow.
4. **Royal Horseguards Thistle Hotel** – Quiet, almost somnambulant restaurant, pricy but discreet.
5. **St Ermine's Hotel** – Used to be known as St Vermins but now revamped. Located by New Scotland Yard, popular with old-school MPs.
6. **Politico's** – Westminster's only political bookstore and coffee house located in Artillery Row. Favourite stop-off for MPs after shopping visit to Army and Navy department store on Victoria Street.
7. **Vitello D'Oro** – Humdrum, cheap Italian restaurant underneath Church House in Great Smith Street. Only place secretaries and researchers can afford to eat outside House of Commons, hence not so popular with MPs.
8. **Red Lion pub** – Downmarket watering-hole opposite Downing Street on Whitehall. Popular with those politicians partial to a bender.
9. **Churchill's** – Pack 'em in, serve 'em quick sandwich bar on Whitehall.
10. **Queen Anne's Restaurant** – Misleading name for Italian restaurant halfway up Victoria Street. Humdrum food and eccentric service.

Ten Politicians with Odd Hobbies

1. Harry Greenway – parachuting
2. Audrey Wise – rearing chickens
3. Edwina Currie – rifle shooting
4. Dennis Skinner – heel and toe walking

5. Ken Livingstone – collecting newts
6. John MacGregor – performing magic tricks
7. Edward Heath – sailing and conducting (but not at the same time)
8. Kenneth Clarke – bird watching
9. Robin Cook – writing 'Tipsters' column in *Sporting Life*
10. Anthony Steen – connoisseur of fine teas

Ten Politicians Who Have Appeared in TV or Newspaper Adverts

1. David Amess (Bananarama's Greatest Hits)
2. Norman St John Stevas (Bananarama's Greatest Hits)
3. Ken Livingstone (National Dairy Council Cheese)
4. Ted Heath (National Dairy Council Cheese)
5. David Steel (Nat West)
6. Cyril Smith (Access)
7. Ronald Reagan (General Electric)
8. Lord George Brown (Normandy Ferries)
9. Clement Freud (Minced Morsels)
10. Ron Brown (Bananarama's Greatest Hits)

Top Ten Political Movies

1. *Paris By Night*
2. *Dave*
3. *Bob Roberts*
4. *JFK*
5. *Nixon*
6. *Damage*
7. *An American President*
8. *Reds*
9. *Washington Behind Closed Doors*
10. *Independence Day*

Twenty Football Clubs with Political Supporters

Brentford – Ann Keen
Celtic – Brian Wilson
Chelsea – John Major, David Mellor, Tony Banks
Everton – Steve Norris, Alan Simpson
Falkirk – Doug Henderson
Hearts – George Foulkes
Leeds United – James Clappison
Manchester United – Tom Pendry
Motherwell – Ann Taylor
Newcastle United – Tony Blair
Nottingham Forest – Kenneth Clarke
Plymouth Argyle – Michael Foot
Port Vale – Joan Walley
Sheffield Wednesday – Roy Hattersley
Stockport County – Peter Snape
Sunderland – Hilary Armstrong
Swansea City – Michael Howard
Swindon Town – Nigel Jones
West Ham – Mike Gapes
York City – John Greenway

Twenty Nicknames for Margaret Thatcher

1. Thatcher – Milk Snatcher – the *Sun*
2. Heather – *Private Eye*
3. Mother – Tory MPs
4. Grocer's Daughter – Valéry Giscard d'Estaing
5. Man with tits – Maureen Colquhoun MP
6. Plutonium Blonde – Arthur Scargill
7. David Owen in drag – *Rhodesia Herald*
8. That Bloody Woman – various
9. Nanny of the nation – Germaine Greer
10. Old iron knickers – Ron Brown
11. The old cow – Richard Needham MP
12. Wicked witch of the west – Gerald Kaufman
13. Thieving magpie – Gerald Kaufman
14. Thatchertollah – Neil Kinnock
15. The Blessed Margaret – Norman St John Stevas

16. The immaculate misconception – Norman St John Stevas
17. Attilla the Hen from Number 10 – Arthur Scargill
18. Bargain Basement Boadicea – Denis Healey
19. TINA (There Is NO Alternative) – *Private Eye*
20. Baroness Belgrano – Edward Pearce

Top Thirty Political Nicknames

Hezza – Michael Heseltine
Tarzan – Michael Heseltine
RAB – R A Butler
Chingford Skinhead – Norman Tebbit
Chips – Henry Channon
Cruella de Ville – Edwina Currie
Comeback Kid – Bill Clinton
Slick Willie – Bill Clinton
Supermac – Harold Macmillan
Shagger – Steve Norris
Boneless Wonder – Ramsay MacDonald
Boy David – David Steel
Hatterji – Roy Hattersley
Ms Hairperson – Harriet Harman
Dr Death – David Owen
Woy – Roy Jenkins
Welsh Windbag – Neil Kinnock
Supergrass – Ian Gow
Minister for Fun – David Mellor
Mogadon Man – Sir Geoffrey Howe
Biffo – John Biffen
Biffo – Geoffrey Dickens (said to stand for Bloody Ignorant Fool From Oldham!)
Lord Suit – Lord Young of Graffham
Afghan Ron – Ron Brown
Paddy Pantsdown – Paddy Ashdown
Red Ken – Ken Livingstone
Sunny Jim – James Callaghan
Worzel Gummidge – Michael Foot
Gum Gum – John Gummer
The Lip – Helmut Schmidt

Fourteen Names Denis Healey called Margaret Thatcher

Catherine the Great of Finchley
Great She Elephant
La Passionaria of Privilege
Rambona
Rhoda the Rhino
Winston Churchill in drag
The lady with the blowlamp
Pétain in petticoats
Castro of the Western World
Calamity Jane
Dragon Empress
Miss Floggie
The Incredible Revolving Maggie
The parrot on Ronald Reagan's shoulder

Tony Blair's New Year's Resolutions

1. Take more notice of that Harman woman's ass
2. Not to worry about the hair loss – no, really
3. To use more verbs
4. Occasionally to disagree with Peter Mandelson
5. To ditch that plank Dobson
6. Tell people to 'Call me Anthony'
7. Improve approval ratings to 110%
8. Hand William Hague a baby's dummy at PM's Questions and tell him to 'Go suck on it'
9. Do something about the Ford Galaxy
10. Buy some new brown paper bags – if you get my meaning

Ten Signs Tony Blair Thinks He's Margaret Thatcher

1. Wanders round Number Ten shrieking 'Rejoice, rejoice'
2. Keeps calling Alastair Campbell Bernard

3. Keeps a close check on Euan's bank account
4. Keeps pouring gin and tonic down Cherie's neck
5. Describes Peter Mandelson as 'One of Them' as opposed to 'One of Us'
6. After Lords defeat on fox hunting announces 'I fight on. I fight to win'
7. Tells close confidant that 'Every Prime Minister needs a Peter'
8. Gazes lovingly into US President's eyes at summit meeting
9. Upon meeting Boris Yeltsin declares: 'I like Mr Yeltsin. We can do business together'
10. Following Prescott's resignation bewilderingly describes him in interview with Brian Walden as 'unassailable'

Ten Ways to Raise Money for the Conservative Party

1. Put condom machine in Opposition whips office
2. Send Virginia Bottomley out to work, if you get my drift
3. Make a quick £3 million by renaming Party 'Big Mac Conservative Party'
4. Open Margaret Thatcher Theme Park on former site of Central Office . . . on second thoughts
5. Cosy up to Asil Nadir
6. Sell off excess supplies of Cecil Parkinson Brylcreem
7. Win the lottery
8. Set light to Michael Heseltine and claim on the insurance
9. Hold a sponsored 'lie a thon'
10. Pay Neil and Christine to shut the f*** up

Tony Blair's Worst Nightmares

1. Answering the phone and hearing 'Hi Tone, it's the Scouse Git here'
2. Waking up and finding 1 May 1997 was an April Fool's joke, one month late
3. At one of his 'Talk to Tony' meetings the whole audience consists of Jeremy Paxman
4. Running out of Chianti
5. Forgetting the word 'new'
6. Something involving Prescott and a sheep
7. Neil Kinnock makes speech hinting at return to British politics
8. John Smith makes surprise guest appearance on X Files
9. David Blunkett abolishes grant maintained schools
10. Cherie is made redundant

Ten Signs John Redwood Is Trying to Be Human

1. Loosens tie during foreplay
2. Appears on *Kilroy* minus trousers
3. Starts hanging around with Gary Barlow
4. Rollerblades to the Commons
5. Shows off *Star Trek* video collection during *Through the Keyhole* with Lloyd Grossman
6. Willing to suffer a repeat humiliation from Clive Anderson
7. Appears on the *Mrs Merton Show* in string vest
8. Refuses to use the words 'logical' and 'captain' in the same sentence
9. Trades in Jag for a Ford Ka
10. Encourages wife to ditch cushy British Airways legal job for trolley dolly vacancy

Ten Signs Cherie Booth Thinks She's Hillary Clinton

1. She expresses a desire to personally reform the National Health Service
2. She denies murdering the Attorney General

3. Always got a downer on Chelsea
4. Looks at her husband in that doe-eyed kind of a way
5. Holds hands with her husband in public
6. Goes pale at Tony's suggestion for a whitewater rafting holiday
7. Wears a badge saying 'Proud to be a Lawyer'
8. Urges Tony to get a tattoo down below just like Bill's
9. Puts phone down upon hearing the words: 'Hi, I'm Paula Jones'
10. Doesn't like these secret meetings with a blonde called Margaret

Ten Politicians Who Have Appeared on *Have I Got News For You*

1. Roy Hattersley
2. Edwina Currie
3. Jerry Hayes
4. Cecil Parkinson
5. Nigel Lawson
6. Diane Abbott
7. Neil Hamilton
8. Neil Kinnock
9. Ken Livingstone
10. Tony Banks

Ten Ways to Let a Twenty-point Opinion Poll Lead Slip

1. Make a speech on how we should give the Falklands to Argentina after all
2. Hire Mr Blobby as your campaign manager
3. Appear on *Noel's House Party* receiving a massage from Julian Clary
4. Sanction special guest appearance by Peter Tatchell at final campaign rally
5. Appear on *Breakfast with Frost* and announce an alliance with Paddy Ashdown
6. Authorise photo opportunity at local swimming baths with Prescott and Hattersley
7. Be filmed leaving Thatcher house by the back door after secret tryst
8. Change your name to George Herbert Walker Bush
9. Authorise sending of free CD of 'Cliff's Greatest Hits' to all first-time voters
10. Appear at Sheffield campaign rally shouting; 'all right, all right, all right' in a Welsh accent

Ten Rejected Titles for John Major's Memoirs

1. 'Nice, Nicer, Nicest'
2. 'Six and Out'
3. 'Fade to Grey'
4. 'Nice Peas'
5. 'Who'd Have Thought It?'
6. 'Serves the Bastards Right'
7. 'Me and the Flapping White Coats'
8. 'A Not Inconsiderable Memoir'
9. 'Memoirs of the Eighth Longest-serving Prime Minister This Century, Oh Yes'
10. 'Tough Luck Rory Bremner'

Ten Things Overheard at the Parliamentary Picnics

1. Prescott sure looks good in those cycling shorts.
2. No Miss Widdecombe, you don't put the potato sack over your head – on second thoughts . . .
3. Isn't that Chris Smith and Ben Bradshaw slow dancing?
4. Put your pants on Mr Ashdown.
5. Could I have another tax-payer subsidised sausage roll, please?
6. I could think of another use for that wicker hamper . . .
7. Shame Neil and Christine couldn't be here.
8. When I said let's put the rug down I wasn't referring to Michael Fabricant.
9. Shame Hague couldn't be here – guess it's past his bedtime.
10. I don't think that's what you're supposed to do with the egg mayonnaise Lord Parkinson.

Ten Unbelievable Political Headlines

1. Thatcher Challenges for Leadership
2. Pitchforks for Iraq Scandal
3. Hague Borrows Fabricant's Hair

4. Blair Steps Down in Favour of Prescott
5. Neil Hamilton to Host *Call my Bluff*
6. Mandelson Says No to Free TV Coverage
7. Taxes Fall Under Labour
8. Tories Pledge 30% Health-spending Rise
9. Jonathan Dimbleby Blasts Patten
10. Tories Odds on to Win Next Election

Thirty-four Celebrities Who Support the Conservatives

Bill Roache (Ken Barlow
   in *Coronation Street*)
Steve Davis
Fred Trueman
Terry Neil
Lynsey de Paul
Sharon Davies
Brian Jacks
Neil Adams
Emlyn Hughes
Jimmy Greaves
Ken Dodd
Jack Walker
Duncan Goodhew
Ian Botham
Bob Monkhouse
Jim Davidson
Jimmy Tarbuck

Cilla Black
Tony Cottee
Nick Faldo
Janet Brown
Ronnie Corbett
Adam Faith
Clive Lloyd
Judith Chalmers
Stan Boardman
Errol Brown
Zandra Rhodes
Bryan Forbes
Nanette Newman
Suzanne Dando
Bob Champion
Michael Winner
Sir Peregrine Worsthorne

Twenty Celebrities Who Support Labour

Pat Nevin	Ben Elton
Tom Watts	Jo Brand
Melvyn Bragg	Hugh Laurie
Billy Bragg	Alan Sillitoe
Neil Pearson	Geraldine Bedell
Brian Clough	Hunter Davies
Alex Ferguson	Christopher Haskins
Kevin Keegan	Nigella Lawson
Richard Wilson	John Mortimer
Stephen Fry	Ken Loach

Eight Celebrities Who Support the Liberal Democrats

John Cleese	Peter Ustinov
Ludovic Kennedy	Brenda Maddox
Edward Woodward	Barry Norman
Barry Took	Nicholas Parsons

Eight Famous Political Marriages

John Maples and Jane Corbin (Tory MP and BBC journalist)

Keith Hampson and Sue Cameron (Tory MP and Channel Four presenter)

Michael Howard and Sandra Paul (Tory MP and former model)

Senator John Warner and Elizabeth Taylor (US Senator and British actress)

Michael Foot and Jill Craigie (Labour politician and authoress)

Gordon and Bridget Prentice (Labour MP and Labour MP)

Alan and Ann Keen (Labour MP and Labour MP)

Andrew Mackay and Julie Kirkbride (Tory MP and Tory MP)

Eight Occasions When Politicians Have Cried in Public

Mrs Thatcher (when Mark was lost in the desert)
Mrs Thatcher (during an interview with Michael Brunson)
Mrs Thatcher (during an interview with Miriam Stoppard)
Bob Hawke (when he admitted being unfaithful to his wife)
Senator Ed Muskie (when asked about his wife's drinking)
President Ford (when congratulating Jimmy Carter on his victory in 1980)
Representative Pat Schroder (announcing that she would not run for President in 1988)
Benazir Bhutto (voting for herself in 1988)

Seven Actor Politicians

Shirley Temple   Nana Mouskouri
Sony Bono   Charlton Heston
Andrew Faulds   Clint Eastwood
Glenda Jackson

Ten Famous Political Homes

The Binns – Tam Dalyell
The Hirsel – Sir Alec Douglas-Home
Blair House – home of the US Vice President
Chequers – country residence of the Prime Minister
Chevening – country residence of the Foreign Secretary
Dorneywood – country residence of the Chancellor of the Exchequer
Cliveden – home of the Astor family
Admiralty House – used by Prime Ministers when 10 Downing Street is unavailable
Camp David – Presidential retreat in Maryland's Catoctin Mountains, originally built in 1942 by President Roosevelt
Chartwell – home of Winston Churchill

Ten Alternative Jobs for Politicians

1. Tony Blair – actor in a Colgate advert
2. John Major – actor in a black and white movie
3. Alan Clark – sperm donor
4. William Hague – Peter Pan
5. John Prescott – Telly Tubby
6. Margaret Hodge – clothes horse
7. Andrew Smith – Dalek replacement
8. Robin Cook – garden gnome
9. Tony Banks – Pearly King
10. Margaret Beckett – Number 3 in the 3.30 at Newmarket

Ten Politicians' Names for Voters

1. Dipsticks
2. Potential shags
3. The enfranchised ones
4. Those whom we serve
5. Those who know not what they do
6. The bosses
7. The little people
8. Ordinary people
9. The bribable masses
10. Those who giveth and taketh away

Ten Good Things About Being Prime Minister

1. Every day, your weight in 10ps from the Dartford Tunnel toll-booth
2. It's the second most powerful position in the country – after the editor of the *Sun*
3. Full control of the nuclear arsenal, aimed at a country of your prejudice
4. You're not married to Anne Heseltine

5. Being able to visit high school gymnasiums at a time of your choice
6. People always telling you what you want to hear
7. Being able to spend, spend, spend
8. You finally get to settle all those scores
9. Subscription-free access to CNN
10. Speeding through red lights in a chauffeur-driven Daimler

Ten Good Things About Being Deputy Prime Minister

1. All the fun with none of the responsibility
2. Allowed to pick any voter at random and spend their taxes on whatever you like
3. You're not married to Cherie
4. Get to pretend to be PM when Tony's away
5. Er, that's it

Ten Signs Tony Blair Has Become 'Hip'

1. Loosens tie during intimate game with Cherie
2. Opens Prime Minister's Questions with 'Awright Will?'
3. He's been shooting the shit with Liam Gallacher
4. Cherie's knackered, if you get the drift
5. Recently seen tapping foot to a Sister Sledge CD
6. Heard screaming abuse at the referee at a Newcastle soccer game
7. Tells Bill Clinton he inhaled
8. Swaps Ford Galaxy people mover for Audi Cabriolet
9. Annoys the neighbours with Def Leppard guitar impersonation
10. Repaints Number Ten door in turquoise

Ten Things You'd Love to Hear Politicians Say But Never Will

1. Margaret Thatcher: I was wrong
2. Tony Blair: I'll never smile again
3. Gerry Adams: I unreservedly condemn the IRA's bombing
4. Norman Lamont: *Je regrette tout*
5. Michael Heseltine: I've given up hope of being Prime Minister
6. Reverend Ian Paisley: And top of the morning to you Mr Adams
7. Alex Salmond: Scotland could never survive on its own
8. Ted Heath: Margaret, I apologise
9. Neil Kinnock: I'm as jealous as hell
10. Teresa Gorman: I can't wait to spend my Euros

Ten Ways of Knowing When a Politician Is Telling a Lie

1. His lips are moving
2. He doesn't look you in the eye
3. He repeats himself
4. He drums his fingers
5. Liberal use of the word 'er'
6. His bald patch starts to sweat
7. Starts telling you the question you ought to be asking him
8. Slags off his opponents
9. Immediately launches into defence of his Party's record regardless of the question
10. Foot tapping turns into St Vitus' Dance

Ten Reasons to Vote for the Green Party

1. You have a beard
2. It's more meaningful than voting Liberal Democrat
3. You work for a sandal manufacturer
4. That Sarah Parkinson seemed such a nice lady
5. You feel guilty for buying that extra gallon of 4 star for your 5 litre Pontiac Trans Am

6. You feel as a vegetarian it's your duty
7. At least they believe what they're saying, even if it is complete balls
8. You've always wanted to till the land
9. You feel sorry for them
10. Someone ought to

Twelve Translations for the Politically Incorrect

1. *Class warfare:* Nicking a ham roll from Asda
2. *Elitist:* Someone who owns a bigger house than you do
3. *Fascist:* Someone who you don't agree with
4. *Bourgeois:* Anyone who shops at Laura Ashley
5. *Tory press:* Fails to report your press release on the Newham Labour Party coffee morning
6. *Sexist:* Watching *Girls on Top*
7. *Racist:* Failing to watch *Desmond's*
8. *Culturally dispossessed:* Anyone who reads Jeffrey Archer novels
9. *Person of gender:* A babe
10. *Pro-choice:* In favour of killing babies
11. *Temporally Challenged:* Shirley Williams
12. *Career Change Opportunity:* You're fired

Forty-one Translations of Things Politicians Say

1.	My good friend ..	Someone who is not a sworn enemy
2.	Freedom fighter	Terrorist whose aims I agree with
3.	Terrorist	Freedom fighter whose aims I disagree with
4.	Courageous	Politically stupid
5.	Divisive	Any policy put forward by the opposition
6.	I'm not a crook	I am a crook
7.	Our European partners	Those wogs over the channel who are trying to screw us
8.	The Right Honourable Member	That prat over the other side
9.	Environmentalists	Sandal-wearing tree-huggers
10.	I did not mean to imply	I certainly did mean to imply
11.	I take full responsibility	My civil servants should take full responsibility
12.	Freedom of the individual	Freedom to infringe the rights of other individuals
13.	In the national interest	In my Party's interest
14.	Read my lips	But I don't really mean it
15.	Urban renewal	Pouring public money into a bottomless pit
16.	Tax cut	Election bribe
17.	Rumour	It must be true
18.	Special relationship	One which allows the Americans to do what they want
19.	Poverty	Owning a black and white television
20.	This will create a dangerous precedent	We might have to do it again
21.	Decentralisation of government	Moving government agencies to marginal seats
22.	It's not the money, it's the principle	It's the money
23.	It's a question of priorities	And our priority right now is not to do it
24.	Few people are likely to be affected	Many people will be affected

25.	I've been quoted out of context	I wish I'd never said it
26.	I said it off the record	I really wish I'd never said it
27.	We are examining all the possibilities	To wheedle our way out of it
28.	Measures will be enacted within the lifetime of this Parliament	We're putting it off indefinitely
29.	We're on course	We're in terrible trouble
30.	That is a simplistic view	It's true but I'm not going to admit it
31.	Full and frank exchange	Blazing row
32.	Businesslike talks	Heated and determined exchange
33.	Frank	Shouting match
34.	Constructive	Polite but without agreement
35.	Let me say this	Listen carefully, I'm about to tell a lie
36.	No disrespect, but	I'm going to insult you
37.	Emerging nation	Backward country run by natives
38.	Active defence	Invasion
39.	Plausible denial	Official lying
40.	Temporarily unsalaried	Unemployed
41.	Advanced defence condition	War

Ten Things you Should Never Say If You Meet Bill Clinton

1. Hello, I'm Gennifer Flowers
2. Hello, I'm Paula Jones
3. How's the tattoo?
4. So, how exactly did Vince Foster die?
5. So, what was Vietnam really like?
6. Have you ever got off with Madeleine Albright?
7. Mr President, I feel your pain
8. John Major just loves to watch Chelsea score
9. Do you want to go whitewater rafting?
10. Name me ten things you and Ted Kennedy have in common

Bibliography

Ash, Russell, *Top Ten of Everything*, Dorling Kindersley, 1996

Butler and Butler, *British Political Facts 1900–94*, Macmillan, 1994

Campaign Guide 1997, Conservative Central Office

Comfort, Nicholas, *Brewer's Politics*, Cassell, 1995

Cook, Chris, *World Political Almanac*, Facts on File, 1995

Cook and Paxton, *European Political Facts 1918–90*, Macmillan, 1991

Dale, Iain, *As I Said to Denis*, Robson Books, 1997

— , *The Blair Necessities*, Robson Books, 1997

Dod's Parliamentary Companion

Englefield, Seaton and White, *Facts about British Prime Ministers*, Mansell, 1995

Foote, Geoffrey, *Chronology of Post War British Politics*, Croom Helm, 1988

Jay, Anthony, *Dictionary of Political Quotations*, Oxford University Press, 1995

Koski and Symons, *You Magazine Book of Journalists*, Chapman, 1990

Letterman, David, *Roman Numeral Two*, Pocket, 1991

McKie, David, *Guardian Political Almanac 1994–5*, Fourth Estate, 1995

Palmer, Alan, *Who's Who in World Politics*, Routledge,, 1996

Parris, Matthew, *Read My Lips*, Robson Books, 1996

—, *Great Parliamentary Scandals*, Robson, 1995

—, *Scorn*, Hamish Hamilton, 1993

Roth, Andrew, *Parliamentary Profiles*, various editions

Ryan, Franklin, *Ronald Reagan The Great Communicator*, Ryan, 1995

Times Guides to the House of Commons, various editions, 1950–97

Vacher's Parliamentary Companion

Waller, Robert, *Almanac of British Politics*, Routledge, 1996

Whitehall Companion, DPR Publishing, 1996